SPANISH PHRASES

FOR BEGINNERS

GAIL STEIN

Publisher Mike Sanders
Editor Christopher Stolle
Designer William Thomas
Compositor Ayanna Lacey
Technical Editor Linda Ruggeri
Proofreader Linda Ruggeri
Indexer Celia McCoy

First American Edition, 2021
Published in the United States by DK Publishing
6081 E. 82nd Street, Indianapolis, Indiana 46250

Copyright © 2021 by Gail Stein
21 22 23 24 25   10 9 8 7 6 5 4 3 2 1
001-322007-FEB2021

Published in the United States by Dorling Kindersley Limited.

ISBN: 978-1-6156-4983-9
Library of Congress Catalog Number: 2020941361

Note: This publication contains the opinions and ideas of its authors. It is intended to provide helpful and informative material on the subject matter covered. It is sold with the understanding that the author(s) and publisher are not engaged in rendering professional services in the book. If the reader requires personal assistance or advice, a competent professional should be consulted. The authors and publisher specifically disclaim any responsibility for any liability, loss, or risk, personal or otherwise, which is incurred as a consequence, directly or indirectly, of the use and application of any of the contents of this book.

Trademarks: All terms mentioned in this book that are known to be or are suspected of being trademarks or service marks have been appropriately capitalized. Alpha Books, DK, and Penguin Random House LLC cannot attest to the accuracy of this information. Use of a term in this book should not be regarded as affecting the validity of any trademark or service mark.
DK books are available at special discounts when purchased in bulk for sales promotions, premiums, fund-raising, or educational use. For details, contact SpecialSales@dk.com.

Printed and bound in the United States

All images © Dorling Kindersley Limited
For further information see: www.dkimages.com

For the curious
www.dk.com

Contents

Dedication

This book is dedicated to my adorable Stein grandchildren: Francesca, Theresa, and Julian. Special thanks to my incredibly supportive editor, Christopher Stolle.

Introduction

Spanish is everywhere. Although I've geared this newly revised edition toward travelers, you're likely to encounter Spanish in familiar and in unknown or foreign places. This book is a great way to learn the words, phrases, and expressions that will not only help you be understood but also allow you to understand others. Whether you're heading to a Spanish-speaking country or your local bodega, you'll appreciate the advantages a knowledge of Spanish can bring you.

What's Inside

You'll learn pronunciation and grammar painlessly and effortlessly without sacrificing speed and accuracy. Whether you're a student, a traveler, or a businessperson, this book will teach you the basics while giving you the vocabulary and the phrases you'll find most useful in almost every conceivable daily situation. You'll be introduced to a wide variety of topics: food, clothing, sports, health, social media, and much more.

This book isn't merely a phrase book, a grammar text, or a travel companion—it's a combination. That makes it not only unique but also an extremely useful tool for people who want a working command of the Spanish language. It will allow you to understand and to be understood without embarrassment or frustration and with ease and enjoyment. Yes, learning Spanish can be fun!

This book was written with you in mind. That's why it's so user-friendly. By the time you've read through it, you'll be a pro at ordering a meal to suit your diet, watching a Spanish film without depending on the subtitles, finding the perfect dance partner, dealing with security personnel before they perform a full-body search at the airport, getting the biggest bang for your bucks, and getting help in an emergency. You'll be amazed and surprised at how rapidly you'll learn what you need to know.

Quick Pronunciation Guide

Spanish has many regional variations. You might hear vocabulary and pronunciation differences, but they're all understandable and intelligible to native speakers.

Diacritical Marks

Mark	Significance	Examples
´ (acute accent)	Put more stress on the vowel.	*árbol* AHR-bohl *él* ehl *frío* FREE-yoh *dónde* DOHN-deh *tú* too

~ (tilde)	Use only with an *n*. Pronounce it like "ny," like in "union."	*mañana* mah-NYAH-nah *niño* NEE-nyoh
¨ (diaeresis)	Sometimes used when *u* is followed by *e* or *i*. Pronounce each vowel separately.	*ambigüedad* ahm-bee-goo-weh-DAHD *lingüista* leen-goo-WEE-stah

Stress

If a word doesn't have an accent mark, where you put the stress depends on several factors:

- If a word ends in a vowel, an *n*, or an *s*, place the stress on the next-to-last syllable.

- If a word ends in any other letter, stress the last syllable.

llama	YAH-mah
examen	ehk-SAH-mehn
casas	KAH-sahs
ciudad	see-yoo-DAHD
hablar	ah-BLAHR

Vowels

a	ah	*Ana*	AH-nah
e	eh	*entrar*	ehn-TRAHR
i	ee	*idea*	ee-DEH-yah
o	oh	*oficina*	oh-fee-SEE-nah
u	oo	*usar*	oo-SAHR

Diphthongs and Vowel Combinations

ae	ahy	*aeropuerto*	ahy-roh-PWEHR-toh
ai	ahy	*aire*	AHY-reh
au	ow	*auto*	OW-toh
ay	ahy	*hay*	ahy
ea	eh-yah	*reacción*	rreh-yahk-see-YOHN
ei	ehy	*beisból*	behys-BOHL
eo	eh-yoh	*feo*	FEH-yoh
eu	eh-yoo	*Europa*	eh-yoo-ROH-pah
ey	ehy	*rey*	rrehy
ia	ee-yah	*Gloria*	GLOH-ree-yah
ie	ee-yeh	*fiesta*	fee-YEHS-tah
io	ee-yoh	*avión*	ah-bee-YOHN
iu	ee-yoo	*ciudad*	see-yoo-DAHD
oa	oh-wah	*toalla*	toh-WAH-yah
oe	oh-weh	*oeste*	oh-WEHS-teh
oi	oy	*oiga*	OY-gah
oy	oy	*soy*	soy
ua	wah	*guardar*	gwahr-DAHR
ue	weh	*cuesta*	KWEHS-tah
ui	wee	*cuidado*	kwee-DAH-doh
uo	oo-oh	*cuota*	koo-OH-tah
uy	wee	*muy*	mwee

Consonants

b	b	*bueno*	BWEH-noh
c	soft c (s) (before e, i)	*centro*	SEHN-troh
	hard c (k) (elsewhere)	*casa*	KAH-sah
ch	ch	*Chile*	CHEE-leh

continues

d	d	*dos*	dohs
f	f	*favor*	fah-BOHR
g	soft g (before e, i)	*general*	heh-neh-RAHL
	hard g (elsewhere)	*gracias*	GRAH-see-yahs
h	silent	*hombre*	OHM-breh
j	h (breathy)	*junto*	HOON-toh
k	k	*kilo*	KEE-loh
l	l	*lista*	LEES-tah
ll	y	*llama*	YAH-mah
m	m	*madre*	MAH-dreh
n	n	*nada*	NAH-dah
ñ	ny	*año*	AH-nyoh
p	p	*padre*	PAH-dreh
q	k	*Quito*	KEE-toh
r	r (small roll)	*salero*	sah-LEH-roh
rr	r (large roll)	*carro*	KAH-rroh
s	s	*sí*	see
t	t	*toro*	TOH-roh
v	b (less explosive English b)	*vender*	behn-DEHR
x	s (followed by consonant)	*extra*	EHS-trah
	ks (followed by vowel)	*exacto*	ehk-SAHK-toh
z	s	*zoo*	soh

Spanish You Already Know

Your knowledge of Spanish is undoubtedly more extensive than you realize. The list of Spanish words used in English is surprisingly long. Here are some English words borrowed from Spanish: chocolate, mosquito, plaza, patio, breeze, stampede, avocado, cargo, vanilla, lasso, canyon, tornado, rancho, tango, siesta. The lists on the following pages give you even more easily recognizable words.

Cognates

A cognate is a foreign word spelled the same or almost the same as a word in English and that has the same meaning. Sometimes, English has actually borrowed words from Spanish (letter for letter) and then they've become part of the English language. Cognates are pronounced differently in each language, but the meaning of the Spanish word is quite obvious to anyone who speaks English.

The following lists of nouns and adjectives provide you with cognates you might find useful. Keep these gender rules in mind:

- Nouns preceded by *el* are masculine singular.
- Nouns preceded by *la* are feminine singular.
- Adjectives ending in *-o* are masculine singular.
- Adjectives ending in *-a* are feminine singular.

Exact Cognates

Masculine Nouns	
el animal	ehl ah-nee-MAHL
el cable	ehl KAH-bleh
el cereal	ehl seh-reh-YAHL
el chocolate	ehl choh-koh-LAH-teh
el color	ehl koh-LOHR
el doctor	ehl dohk-TOHR
el hospital	ehl ohs-pee-TAHL
el hotel	ehl oh-TEHL
el mosquito	ehl mohs-KEE-toh
el motor	ehl moh-TOHR
el taxi	ehl TAHK-see
Feminine Nouns	
la banana	lah bah-NAH-nah
la idea	lah ee-DEH-yah
la plaza	lah PLAH-sah
la radio	lah RRAH-dee-yoh
Adjectives	
natural	nah-too-RAHL
popular	poh-poo-LAHR
probable	proh-BAH-bleh

Almost Exact Cognates

These words have slightly different spellings than their English counterparts, but just like with exact cognates, their meanings are easily understood.

Masculine Nouns	
el *aniversario*	ehl ah-nee-behr-SAH-ree-yoh
el *automóvil*	ehl ow-toh-MOH-beel
el *banco*	ehl BAHN-koh
el *celular*	ehl seh-loo-LAHR
el *diccionario*	ehl deek-see-yoh-NAH-ree-yoh
el *mecánico*	ehl meh-KAH-nee-koh
el *menú*	ehl meh-NOO
el *móvil*	ehl MOH-beel
el *parque*	ehl PAHR-keh
el *plato*	ehl PLAH-toh
el *programa*	ehl proh-GRAH-mah
el *restaurante*	ehl rrehs-TOW-rahn-teh
el *supermercado*	ehl soo-pehr-mehr-KAH-doh
el *teatro*	ehl teh-YAH-troh
el *teléfono*	ehl teh-LEH-foh-noh
Feminine Nouns	
la *aspirina*	lah ahs-pee-REE-nah
la *bicicleta*	lah bee-see-KLEH-tah
la *blusa*	lah BLOO-sah
la *cathedral*	lah kah-teh-DRAHL
la *computadora*	lah kohm-poo-tah-DOH-rah
la *familia*	lah fah-MEE-lyah
la *hamburguesa*	lah ahm-boor-GEH-sah
la *medicina*	lah meh-dee-SEE-nah
la *música*	lah MOO-see-kah

continues

la persona	lah pehr-SOH-nah
la turista	lah too-REES-tah
Adjectives	
americano(a)	ah-meh-ree-KAH-noh (nah)
confortable	kohn-fohr-TAH-bleh
delicioso(a)	deh-lee-see-YOH-soh (sah)
diferente	dee-feh-REHN-teh
difícil	dee-FEE-seel
elegante	eh-leh-GAHN-teh
famoso(a)	fah-MOH-soh (sah)
grande	GRAHN-deh
importante	eem-pohr-TAHN-teh
imposible	eem-poh-SEE-bleh
interesante	een-teh-reh-SAHN-teh
moderno(a)	moh-DEHR-noh (nah)
necesario(a)	neh-seh-SAH-ree-yoh (yah)
posible	poh-SEE-bleh

Verbs

Verbs (action words) can also be cognates. Most Spanish verbs fall into one of three categories:

- the -*ar* family
- the -*er* family
- the -*ir* family

These verbs are considered regular because all verbs in the same family follow the same rules.

-*ar* Verb Cognates	
acompañar	ah-kohm-pah-NYAHR
celebrar	seh-leh-BRAHR

entrar	ehn-TRAHR
explicar	ehs-plee-KAHR
invitar	een-bee-TAHR
preparar	preh-pah-RAHR
reservar	rreh-sehr-BAHR
usar	oo-SAHR

-er Verb Cognates

comprender	kohm-prehn-DEHR
responder	rrehs-pohn-DEHR
vender	behn-DEHR

-ir Verb Cognates

| *decidir* | deh-see-DEER |
| *recibir* | rreh-see-BEER |

Chapter 3

The Basics

This chapter gives you the essential words and expressions you'll need for commonplace situations: using numbers, telling time, expressing dates (days of the week, months, the seasons), asking about and expressing the weather, using formal and informal greetings and salutations, being polite, and getting information.

Numbers

Cardinal Numbers

0	*cero* SEH-roh
1	*uno* OO-noh
2	*dos* dohs
3	*tres* trehs
4	*cuatro* KWAH-troh
5	*cinco* SEEN-koh
6	*seis* SEHY-ees
7	*siete* see-YEH-teh
8	*ocho* OH-choh
9	*nueve* NWEH-beh
10	*diez* dee-YEHS
11	*once* OHN-seh
12	*doce* DOH-seh
13	*trece* TREH-seh
14	*catorce* kah-TOHR-seh
15	*quince* KEEN-seh
16	*dieciséis* dee-yehs-ee-SEHY-ees

17	*diecisiete* dee-yehs-ee-see-YEH-teh
18	*dieciocho* dee-yehs-ee-OH-choh
19	*diecinueve* dee-yehs-ee-NWEH-beh
20	*veinte* BEHYN-teh
21	*veintiuno* behyn-tee-OO-noh
22	*veintidós* behyn-tee-DOHS
30	*treinta* TREHYN-tah
40	*cuarenta* kwah-REHN-tah
50	*cincuenta* seen-KWEHN-tah
60	*sesenta* seh-SEHN-tah
70	*setenta* seh-TEHN-tah
80	*ochenta* oh-CHEHN-tah
90	*noventa* noh-BEHN-tah
100	*cien* see-YEHN
101	*ciento uno* see-YEHN-toh OO-noh
200	*doscientos* dohs-see-YEHN-tohs
500	*quinientos* kee-nee-YEHN-tohs
700	*setecientos* seh-teh-see-YEHN-tohs
900	*novecientos* noh-beh-see-YEHN-tohs
1,000	*mil* meel

continues

2,000	*dos mil* dohs meel
100,000	*cien mil* see-YEHN meel
1,000,000	*un millón* oon mee-YOHN
2,000,000	*dos millones* dohs mee-YOH-nehs

Ordinal Numbers

first	*primero* pree-MEH-roh
second	*segundo* seh-GOON-doh
third	*tercero* tehr-SEH-roh
fourth	*cuarto* KWAHR-toh
fifth	*quinto* KEEN-toh
sixth	*sexto* SEHS-toh
seventh	*séptimo* SEHP-tee-moh
eighth	*octavo* ohk-TAH-boh
ninth	*noveno* noh-BEH-noh
tenth	*décimo* DEH-see-moh

In numerals and decimals, wherever Americans use commas, Spanish-speaking people use periods (and vice versa).

English	6,000.75
Spanish	6.000,25

The numbers 16 to 19 and 21 to 29 are generally written as one word. When this is done, the numbers 16, 22, 23, and 26 have accents.

16	22
dieciséis	*veintidós*
17	23
diecisiete	*veintitrés*
21	26
veintiuno	*veintiséis*

They might, however, also be written as two numbers joined by the conjunction *y* (and).

16	22
diez y seis	*veinte y dos*

The conjunction *y* (and) is used only for numbers between 16 and 99.

99	120
noventa y nueve	*ciento veinte*

Uno is used only when counting. It becomes *un* before a masculine noun and *una* before a feminine noun.

uno, dos, tres …
one, two, three …

treinta y un muchachos
thirty-one boys

un hombre y una mujer

a man and a woman

veintiuna muchachas

twenty-one girls

Compounds of *ciento* (*doscientos, tresceintos*) should agree with the feminine noun.

doscientos hombres y trescientas mujeres

two hundred men and three hundred women

Make ordinal numbers feminine by changing the final *-o* of the masculine form to *-a*.

la Quinta Avenida

Fifth Avenue

Primero and *tercero* drop their final *-o* before a masculine singular noun.

el primer mes   *el tercer día*

the first month   the third day

Telling Time

What time is it?	*¿Qué hora es?* keh OH-rah ehs
At what time?	*¿A qué hora?* ah keh OH-rah
It's 1:00.	*Es la una.* ehs lah OO-nah
It's 2:05.	*Son las dos y cinco.* sohn lahs dohs ee SEEN-koh

It's 3:10.	*Son las tres y diez.* sohn lahs trehs ee dee-YEHS
It's 4:15.	*Son las cuatro y cuarto.* sohn lahs KWAH-troh ee KWAHR-toh
It's 5:20.	*Son las cinco y veinte.* sohn lahs SEEN-koh ee BEHYN-teh
It's 6:25.	*Son las seis y veinticinco.* sohn lahs SEHY-ees ee behyn-tee-SEEN-koh
It's 7:30.	*Son las siete y media.* sohn lahs see-YEH-teh ee meh-DEE-yah
It's 7:35. (25 minutes to 8:00)	*Son las ocho menos* *veinticinco.* sohn lahs OH-choh meh-NOHS behyn-tee-SEEN-koh
It's 8:40. (20 minutes to 9:00)	*Son las nueve menos veinte.* sohn lahs NWEH-beh MEH- nohs BEHYN-teh
It's 9:45. (15 minutes to 10:00)	*Son las diez menos cuarto.* sohn lahs dee-YEHS MEH-nohs KWAHR-toh
It's 10:50. (10 minutes to 11:00)	*Son las once menos diez.* sohn lahs OHN-seh MEH-nohs dee-YEHS
It's 11:55. (5 minutes to 12:00)	*Son las doce menos cinco.* sohn lahns DOH-seh MEH- nohs SEEN-koh
It's noon.	*Es el mediodía.* ehs ehl meh-dee-yoh-DEE-yah
It's midnight.	*Es la medianoche.* ehs lah meh-dee-yah-NOH- cheh

It's not unusual to hear the time expressed this way:

> *Son las dos y cuarenta y cinco.*
>
> It's 2:45.

These expressions are helpful when referring to the time in general.

a second	*un segundo* oon seh-GOON-doh
a minute	*un minuto* oon mee-NOO-toh
an hour	*una hora* OO-nah OH-rah
in the morning (a.m.)	*de la mañana* deh lah mah-NYAH-nah
in the afternoon (p.m.)	*de la tarde* deh lah TAHR-deh
in the evening (p.m.)	*de la noche* deh lah NOH-cheh
at what time	*¿a qué hora?* ah keh OH-rah
at exactly 2:00	*a las dos en punto* ah lahs dohs ehn POON-toh
at about	*a eso de* ah EH-soh deh
an hour	*una hora* OO-nah OH-rah
a half hour	*una media hora* OO-nah MEH-dee-yah OH-rah
in an hour	*en una hora* ehn OO-nah OH-rah
until 2:00	*hasta las dos* AHS-tah lahs dohs
before 3:00	*antes de las tres* AHN-tehs deh lahs trehs
after 3:00	*después de las tres* dehs-PWEHS deh lahs trehs
since (from) what time	*desde qué hora* DEHS-deh keh OH-rah
since 6:00	*desde las seis* DEHS-deh lahs SEHY-ees
an hour ago	*hace una hora* AH-seh OO-nah OH-rah

per hour	*por hora* pohr OH-rah
early	*temprano* tehm-PRAH-noh
late	*tarde* TAHR-deh
late (in arriving)	*de retraso* deh rreh-TRAH-soh
on time	*a tiempo* ah tee-YEHM-poh

Days of the Week

In Spanish, the days of the week are only capitalized at the beginning of a sentence. Elsewhere, unlike in English, they're written with a lowercase first letter.

> *Sábado es un día.*

> Saturday is a day.

> *Voy al supermercado el sábado.*

> I go to the supermarket on Saturday.

Monday	*lunes* LOO-nehs
Tuesday	*martes* MAHR-tehs
Wednesday	*miércoles* mee-YEHR-koh-lehs
Thursday	*jueves* HWEH-behs
Friday	*viernes* bee-YEHR-nehs
Saturday	*sábado* SAH-bah-doh
Sunday	*domingo* doh-MEEN-goh

To express "on" when talking about a certain day, use the definite article *el* or *los*.

> *Voy al cine el viernes.*

> I go to the movies on Friday.

> *No trabajo los domingos.*

> I don't work on Sundays.

Months

Like days of the week, unless used at the beginning of a sentence, the names of all months should be written in lowercase.

> *Enero es un mes.*

> January is a month.

> *Voy a España en enero.*

> I go to Spain in January.

January	*enero* eh-NEH-roh
February	*febrero* feh-BREH-roh
March	*marzo* MAHR-soh
April	*abril* AH-breel
May	*mayo* MAH-yoh
June	*junio* HOO-nee-yoh
July	*julio* HOO-lee-yoh

August	*agosto* ah-GOHS-toh
September	*septiembre* sehp-tee-YEHM-breh
October	*octubre* ohk-TOO-breh
November	*noviembre* noh-bee-YEHM-breh
December	*diciembre* dee-see-YEHM-breh

Dates

When you have to refer to a date, use the following.

What day is it (today)?	*¿Qué día es (hoy)?* keh DEE-yah ehs (ohy)
What's today's date?	*¿A cuántos estamos hoy?* ah KWAHN-tohs ehs-TAH-mohs ohy
What's the date today?	*¿Cuál es la fecha (de hoy)?* kwahl ehs lah FEH-chah (deh ohy)

Express the date as follows:

day of the week + *el* + (cardinal) number
+ *de* + month + *de* + year

Hoy es sábado el nueve de mayo de dos mil veinte.

Estamos a sábado el nueve de mayo de dos mil veinte.

Today is Saturday, May 9, 2020.

Use *primero* to express the first of each month.

Es el primero de mayo.

It's May 1st.

Es el veintiuno de mayo.

It's May 21st.

Use the definite article *el* to express "on" with dates.

Me voy el once de julio.

I'm leaving on July 11th.

In Spanish, the date is written by reversing the month/day sequence used in English.

el 14 de septiembre de 1947 (14.9.47)

September 14th, 1947 (9/14/47)

Don't use hundreds, as we do in English, when giving the year.

mil novecientos noventa y nueve

1999

Seasons

autumn, fall	*el otoño* ehl oh-TOH-nyoh
spring	*la primavera* lah pree-mah-BEH-rah
summer	*el verano* ehl beh-RAH-noh
winter	*el invierno* ehl een-bee-YEHR-noh

Weather

What's the weather?	*¿Qué tiempo hace?* keh tee-YEHM-poh AH-seh
It's beautiful.	*Hace buen tiempo.* AH-seh bwehn tee-YEHM-poh
It's hot.	*Hace calor.* AH-seh kah-LOHR
It's sunny.	*Hace sol.* AH-seh sohl
It's nasty (bad).	*Hace mal tiempo.* AH-seh mahl tee-YEHM-poh
It's cold.	*Hace frío.* AH-seh FREE-yoh
It's cool.	*Hace fresco.* AH-seh FREHS-koh
It's windy.	*Hace viento.* AH-seh bee-YEHN-toh
It's lightning.	*Hay relámpagos.* ahy rreh-LAHM-pah-gohs
It's thundering.	*Truena.* TRWEH-nah
It's foggy.	*Hay niebla.* ahy nee-YEH-blah
It's misty.	*Hay neblina.* ahy neh-BLEE-nah
It's humid.	*Hay humedad.* ahy oo-meh-DAHD
It's cloudy.	*Hay nubes.* ahy NOO-behs
	Está nublado. ehs-TAH noo-BLAH-doh
It's overcast.	*Está cubierto.* ehs-TAH koo-bee-YEHR-toh
It's raining.	*Llueve.* YWEH-beh
	Está lloviendo. ehs-TAH yoh-bee-YEHN-doh

continues

It's pouring.	*Hay lluvias torrenciales.* ahy YOO-bee-yahs toh-rrehn-see-YAH-lehs
It's snowing.	*Nieva.* nee-YEH-bah
	Está nevando. ehs-TAH neh-BAHN-doh
There's a windstorm.	*Hay un vendaval.* ahy oon behn-dah-BAHL
There's hail.	*Hay granizo.* ahy grah-NEE-soh
There are showers.	*Hay lluvias.* ahy YOO-bee-yahs

Greetings and Salutations

Formal Salutations

Use these when speaking to someone you don't know well or to whom you should show respect.

Hello/Good morning.	*Buenos días.* BWEH-nohs DEE-yahs
Good afternoon.	*Buenas tardes.* BWEH-nahs TAHR-dehs
Good evening.	*Buenas noches.* BWEH-nahs NOH-chehs
Mister, sir	*Señor* seh-NYOHR
Miss, young woman	*Señorita* seh-nyoh-REE-tah
Mrs., madam, woman	*Señora* seh-NYOH-rah
My name is …	*Me llamo …* meh YAH-moh
What's your name?	*¿Cómo se llama?* KOH-moh seh YAH-mah

How are you?	*¿Cómo está?* KOH-moh EHS-tah
Very well	*Muy bien* mwee bee-YEHN
So-so	*Así así* ah-SEE ah-SEE *Regular* rreh-goo-LAHR
Nice to meet you.	*Mucho gusto.* MOO-choh GOOS-toh
It's a pleasure.	*Es un placer.* ehs oon plah-SEHR
The pleasure is mine.	*El gusto es mío.* ehl GOOS-toh ehs MEE-yoh
Goodbye.	*Adiós.* ah-dee-YOHS
See you tomorrow.	*Hasta mañana.* AHS-tah mah-NYAH-nah

Informal Salutations

An informal opening conversation (between young people or friends) might use these phrases.

Hi!	*¡Hola!* OH-lah
My name is ...	*Me llamo ...* meh YAH-moh
What's your name?	*¿Cómo te llamas?* KOH-moh teh YAH-mahs
How are you?	*¿Cómo estás?* KOH-moh ehs-TAHS
How's it going?	*¿Cómo te va?* KOH-moh teh bah
How are things?	*¿Qué tal?* keh tahl

continues

What's happening?	*¿Qué pasa?* keh PAH-sah
What's new?	*¿Qué hay de nuevo?* keh ahy deh NWEH-boh
Nothing much.	*Nada de particular.* NAH-dah deh pahr-tee-koo-LAHR
See you later.	*Hasta luego.* AHS-tah LWEH-goh
See you soon.	*Hasta pronto.* AHS-tah PROHN-toh
Till I see you again.	*Hasta la vista.* AHS-tah lah BEES-tah
Have a nice day.	*Que te vaya bien.* keh teh BAH-yah bee-YEHN

Being Polite

Please.	*Por favor.* pohr fah-BOHR
Thank you (very much).	*(Muchas) Gracias.* (MOO-chahs) GRAH-see-yahs
Thank you for everything.	*Gracias por todo.* GRAH-see-yahs pohr TOH-doh
You're welcome.	*De nada.* deh NAH-dah
	No hay de qué. noh ahy deh keh
Excuse me.	*Disculpe.* dees-KOOL-peh
	Perdóneme. pehr-DOH-neh-meh
I'm sorry.	*Lo siento.* loh see-YEHN-toh
I'm sorry to bother you.	*Siento molestarle.* see-YEHN-toh moh-lehs-TAHR-leh

If you don't mind.	*Si no le importa.* see noh leh eem-POHR-tah
Bless you! (after sneezing)	*Salud!* sah-LOOD

Getting Information

Use these question words when you want to get
information. Note that all question words have an
accent. The easiest way to ask for information is to
put the question word immediately before the verbal
phrase or thought. In Spanish, an inverted question
mark precedes the question and an upright question
mark follows it.

¿Con quién viajas? kohn kee-YEHN bee-YAH-hahs	With whom are you traveling?
adónde ah-DOHN-deh	to where
a qué hora ah keh OH-rah	at what time
a quién ah kee-YEHN	to whom
a qué ah keh	to what
con quién kohn kee-YEHN	with whom
con qué kohn keh	with what
cuál kwahl	which
de quién deh kee-YEHN	of, about, from whom
de qué deh keh	of, about, from what
cuánto KWAHN-toh	how much, how many

continues

cómo KOH-moh	how
dónde DOHN-deh	where
de dónde deh DOHN-deh	from where
por qué pohr keh	why
cuándo KWAHN-doh	when
quién(es) kee-YEHN (kee-YEH-nehs)	who, whom
qué keh	what

Beginners will find the following phrases useful when giving and getting information are key.

Do you speak English?	*¿Habla inglés?* AH-blah een-GLEHS
Does anyone speak English?	*¿Alguien aquí habla inglés?* ahl-gee-YEHN ah-KEE ah-BLAH een-GLEHS
Do you understand me?	*¿Me entiende?* meh ehn-tee-YEHN-deh
I speak (a little) Spanish.	*Hablo español (un poco).* AH-bloh ehs-pah-NYOHL (oon POH-koh)
I don't speak Spanish.	*No hablo español.* noh AH-bloh ehs-pah-NYOHL
I (don't) understand.	*(No) Comprendo.* (noh) kohm-PREHN-doh *(No) Entiendo.* (noh) ehn-tee-YEHN-doh
I'm confused.	*Estoy confundido(a)* ehs-TOY kon-foon-DEE-doh (dah)
I need an interpreter.	*Necesito un intérprete.* neh-seh-SEE-toh oon een- TEHR-preh-teh

I didn't hear you.	*No le entendí.* noh leh ehn-tehn-DEE
Please speak more slowly.	*Hable más despacio por favor.* AH-bleh mahs dehs-PAH-see-yoh pohr fah-BOHR
Please repeat.	*Repita por favor.* rreh-PEE-tah pohr fah-BOHR
What did you say?	*¿Cómo?* KOH-moh
What does that mean?	*¿Qué significa?* keh seeg-nee-FEE-kah
How do you say … in Spanish?	*¿Cómo se dice … en español?* KOH-moh seh DEE-seh … ehn ehs-pah-NYOHL
Can you write that down?	*¿Puede escribirlo?* PWEH-deh ehs-kree-BEER-loh
How do you spell that?	*¿Cómo se deletrea?* KOH-moh seh deh-leh-TREH-yah
Can you help me?	*¿Puede ayudarme?* PWEH-deh ah-yoo-DAHR-meh
I need help.	*Necesito ayuda.* neh-seh-SEE-toh ah-YOO-dah
I have a problem.	*Tengo un problema.* tehn-GOH oon proh-BLEH-mah
What's this?	*¿Qué es esto?* keh ehs EHS-toh

Personal Profile

In many different situations, you might find it
necessary to convey personal information in
Spanish: your name, nationality, occupation, family
relationships, hobbies, and pastimes. Or perhaps
you'll need or want to participate on social media
sites. This chapter will help you do all this.

Names

My name is …	*Me llamo …* meh YAH-moh *Mi nombre es …* mee NOHM-breh ehs
What's your name?	*¿Cómo se llama?* (polite) KOH-moh seh YAH-mah
What's your name?	*¿Cómo te llamas?* (familiar) KOH-moh teh YAH-mahs
What's your last (maiden) (married last) name?	*¿Cuál es su apellido (de* *soltera) (de casada)?* kwahl ehs soo ah-peh-YEE-doh (deh sohl-TEH-rah) (deh kah- SAH-dah)

Country of Origin
and Nationalities

Where are you from?	*¿De dónde es?* (polite) deh DOHN-deh ehs
Where are you from?	*¿De dónde eres?* (familiar) deh DOHN-deh EH-rehs
I'm (We're) from …	*Soy (Somos) de …* soy (SOH-mohs) (deh)
I'm (We're) …	*Soy (Somos) …* soy (SOH-mohs)

Country		**Nationality**	
Canada	*Canadá* kah-nah-DAH	Canadian	*canadiense(s)* kah-nah-dee- YEHN-see (sehs)
China	*China* CHEE-nah	Chinese	*chino(a)(s)* CHEE-noh (nah) (s)

England	*Inglaterra* een-glah-TEH-rrah	English	*inglés (ingleses),* *inglesa(s)* een-GLEHS (een-GLEH-sehs) een-GLEH-sah(s)
France	*Francia* FRAHN-see-yah	French	*francés* *(franceses),* *francesa(s)* frahn-SEHS (frahn-SEH-sehs), frahn-SEH-sah(s)
Germany	*Alemania* ah-leh-MAH-nee-yah	German	*alemán* *(alemanes),* *alemana(s)* ah-leh-MAHN (ah-leh-MAH-nehs), ah-leh-MAH-nah(s)
Greece	*Grecia* GREH-see-yah	Greek	*griego(a)(s)* gree-YEH-goh (gah)(s)
Ireland	*Irlanda* eer-LAHN-dah	Irish	*irlandés* *(irlandeses),* *irlandesa(s)* eer-lahn-DEHS (eer-lahn-DEH-sehs), eer-lahn-DEH-sah(s)
Italy	*Italia* ee-TAHL-yah	Italian	*italiano(a)(s)* ee-tahl-YAH-noh (nah)(s)
Japan	*Japón* hah-POHN	Japanese	*japonés* *(japoneses),* *japonesa(s)* hah-poh-NEHS (hah-poh-NEH-sehs), hah-poh-NEH-sah(s)
Norway	*Noruega* nohr-WEH-gah	Norwegian	*noruego(a)(s)* noh-RWEH-goh (gah)(s)
Russia	*Rusia* RROO-see-yah	Russian	*ruso(a)(s)* RROO-soh (sah)(s)

continues

Spain	*España* ehs-PAH-nyah	Spanish	*Español (españoles), española(s)* ehs-pah-NYOHL (ehs-pah-NYOH-lehs) ehs-pah-NYOH-lah(s)
Sweden	*Suecia* SWEH-see-yah	Swedish	*sueco(a)(s)* SWEH-koh (kah) (s)
Switzer-land	*Suiza* SWEE-sah	Swiss	*suizo(a)(s)* SWEE-soh (sah) (s)
United States	*los Estados Unidos* lohs ehs-TAH-dohs oo-NEE-dohs	American	*americano(a)(s)* ah-meh-ree-KAH-noh (nah)(s)

Occupations

How do you earn a living?	*¿Cómo se gana la vida?* KOH-moh seh GAH-nah lah BEE-dah
I'm a (an) …	*Soy* … soy
accountant.	*contable.* (m./f.) kohn-TAH-bleh

contador(a) kohn-tah-DOHR (kohn-tah-DOH-rah) |
businessperson.	*persona de negocios.* pehr-SOH-nah deh neh-GOH-see-yohs
computer tech.	*informático(a).* een-fohr-MAH-tee-koh (kah)
dentist.	*dentista.* (m./f.) dehn-TEES-tah
doctor.	*médico(a).* MEH-dee-koh (kah)
engineer.	*ingeniero(a).* een-heh-NYEH-roh (rah)

firefighter.	*bombero(a).* bohm-beh-roh (rah)
government employee.	*empleado(a) del gobierno.* ehm-pleh-YAH-doh (dah) dehl goh-bee-YEHR-noh
hairdresser.	*peluquero(a).* peh-loo-KEH-roh (rah)
jeweler.	*joyero(a).* hoh-YEH-roh (rah)
lawyer.	*abogado(a).* ah-boh-GAH-doh (dah)
nurse.	*enfermero(a).* ehn-fehr-MEH-roh (rah)
police officer.	*agente de policía.* (m./f.) ah-HEHN-teh deh poh-lee-SEE-yah
postal worker.	*curtero(a).* kahr-TEH-roh (rah)
programmer.	*programador(a).* proh-grah-mah-DOHR (DOH-rah)
salesperson.	*vendedor(a).* behn-deh-DOHR (DOH-rah)
secretary.	*secretario(a).* seh-kreh-TAH-ree-yoh (yah)
self-employed.	*autónomo(a).* ow-TOH-noh-moh (mah)
store owner.	*comerciante.* koh-mehr-see-YAHN-teh
student.	*estudiante.* ehs-too-dee-YAHN-teh
teacher.	*profesor(a).* proh-feh-SOHR (SOH-rah)
waiter.	*camarero(a).* kah-mah-REH-roh (rah)
I'm in …	*Estoy en …* ehs-TOY ehn …
the army.	*el ejército.* ehl eh-HEHR-see-toh

continues

the navy.	*la marina.* lah mah-REE-nah
the air force.	*la fuerza aérea.* lah FWEHR-sah AHY-reh-yah
the marines.	*los marines.* lohs mah-REE-nehs
I work part-time.	*Trabajo a tiempo parcial.* trah-BAH-hoh ah tee-YEHM-poh pahr-see-YAHL
I'm semi-retired.	*Estoy semi-retirado(a).* ehs-TOY SEH-mee-rreh-tee-RAH-doh (dah)
I'm retired.	*Estoy jubilado(a).* ehs-TOY hoo-bee-LAH-doh (dah)

Physical Descriptions

What do you look like?	*¿Cómo es?* (polite) KOH-moh ehs
What do you look like?	*¿Cómo eres?* (familiar) KOH-moh EH-rehs
I'm … years old.	*Tengo … años.* TEHN-goh … AH-nyohs
I'm short/tall.	*Soy bajo(a)/alto(a).* soy BAH-hoh (hah)/AHL-toh (tah)
I weigh (about) … pounds (kilograms).	*Peso más o menos … libras (kilogramos).* PEH-soh mahs oh MEH-nohs … LEE-brahs (kee-loh-GRAH-mohs)
I'm … feet … inches (meters) tall.	*Mido … pies … pulgadas (centímetros).* MEE-doh … pee-YEHS … pool-GAH-dahs (sehn-TEE-meh-trohs)
I have … hair.	*Tengo pelo … .* TEHN-goh PEH-loh
short	*corto* KOHR-toh

long	*largo*
	LAHR-goh
straight	*lacio*
	LAH-see-yoh
curly	*rizado*
	rree-SAH-doh
light	*claro*
	KLAH-roh
dark	*oscuro*
	ohs-KOO-roh
blond	*rubio*
	RROO-bee-yoh
brown	*castaño*
	kahs-TAH-nyoh
black	*negro*
	NEH-groh
I have red hair.	*Soy pelirrojo(a).*
	soy peh-lee-RROH-hoh (hah)
I have gray hair.	*Soy canoso(a).*
	soy kah-NOH-soh (sah)
I'm bald.	*Soy calvo(a).*
	soy KAHL-boh (bah)
I have … eyes.	*Tengo ojos … .*
	TEHN-goh OH-hohs
blue	*azules*
	ah-SOO-lehs
brown	*marrones*
	mah-RROH-nehs
dark	*oscuros*
	ohs-KOO-rohs
gray	*grises*
	GREE-sehs
green	*verdes*
	BEHR-dehs
hazel	*de color avellana*
	deh koh-LOHR ah-beh-YAH-nah
light	*claros*
	KLAH-rohs

continues

I have a moustache (beard).	*Tengo un bigote (una barba).* TEHN-goh oon bee-GOH-teh (OO-nah BAHR-bah)
I have a tattoo (tattoos).	*Tengo un tatuaje* *(tatuajes).* TEHN-goh oon tah-TWAH-heh (tah-TWAH-hehs)
I have a piercing (piercings).	*Tengo un piercing* *(piercings).* TEHN-goh oon piercing (piercings).
I'm ...	*Soy ...* soy
single.	*soltero(a).* sohl-TEH-roh (rah)
married.	*casado(a).* kah-SAH-doh (dah)
separated.	*separado(a).* seh-pah-RAH-doh (dah)
divorced.	*divorciado(a).* dee-bohr-see-YAH-doh (dah)
I'm a widow(er).	*Soy viuda(o).* soy bee-YOO-dah (doh)
I have one (two) children.	*Tengo un (dos) niño(s).* TEHN-goh oon (dohs) NEE- nyohs.
I don't have any children.	*No tengo niños.* noh TEHN-goh NEE-nyohs
I have a dog (cat).	*Tengo un perro (gato).* TEHN-goh oon PEH-rroh (GAH- toh)

Personality Traits

I'm ...	*Soy ...* soy
ambitious.	*ambicioso(a).* ahm-bee-see-YOH-soh (sah)
athletic.	*deportivo(a).* deh-pohr-TEE-boh (bah)

courteous.	*cortés.* kohr-TEHS
daring.	*atrevido(a).* ah-treh-BEE-doh (dah)
efficient.	*eficiente.* eh-fee-see-YEHN-teh
extroverted.	*extrovertido(a).* ehs-troh-behr-TEE-doh (dah)
friendly.	*simpático(a).* seem-PAH-tee-koh (kah)
fun.	*divertido(a).* dee-behr-TEE-doh (dah)
funny.	*cómico(a)* KOH-mee-koh (kah)
generous.	*generoso(a).* heh-neh-ROH-soh (sah)
happy.	*alegre.* ah-LEH-greh
honest.	*honrado(a).* ohn-RAH-doh (dah)
impulsive.	*impulsivo(a).* eem-pool-SEE-boh (bah)
introverted.	*introvertido(a).* een-troh-behr-TEE-doh (dah)
nice.	*amable.* ah-MAH-bleh
open.	*abierto(a).* ah-bee-YEHR-toh (tah)
optimistic.	*optimista.* ohp-tee-MEES-tah
pessimistic.	*pesimista.* peh-see-MEES-tah
proud	*orgulloso(a).* ohr-goo-YOH-soh (sah)
punctual.	*puntual.* poon-TWAHL
realistic.	*realista.* rreh-yah-LEES-tah

continues

reasonable.	*razonable.* rrah-soh-NAH-bleh
responsible.	*responsable.* rrehs-pohn-SAH-bleh
shy.	*tímido(a).* TEE-mee-doh (dah)
sincere.	*sincero(a).* seen-SEH-roh (rah)
sociable.	*sociable.* soh-see-YAH-bleh
talkative.	*hablador(a).* ah-blah-DOHR (DOH-rah)

Hobbies and Pastimes

I like to …	*Me gusta …* meh GOOS-tah
cook.	*cocinar.* koh-see-NAHR
dance.	*bailar.* BAHY-lahr
draw.	*dibujar.* dee-boo-HAHR
go running.	*ir a correr.* eer ah koh-RREHR
go shopping.	*ir de compras.* eer deh KOHM-prahs
go to concerts.	*ir a conciertos.* eer ah kohn-see-YEHR-tohs
go to museums.	*ir a museos.* eer ah moo-SEH-yohs
go to the ballet.	*ir al ballet.* eer ahl bah-LEH
go to the beach.	*ir a la playa.* eer ah lah PLAH-yah
go to the movies.	*ir al cine.* eer ahl SEE-neh
go to the opera.	*ir a la ópera.* eer ah lah OH-peh-rah

go to the theater.	*ir al teatro.* eer ahl teh-YAH-troh
knit.	*tejer.* teh-HEHR
listen to music.	*escuchar música.* ehs-koo-CHAHR MOO-see-kah
paint.	*pintar.* peen-TAHR
play cards.	*jugar a los naipes.* hoo-GAHR ah lohs NAHY-pehs
play checkers.	*jugar a las damas.* hoo-GAHR ah lahs DAH-mahs
play chess.	*jugar al ajedrez.* hoo-GAHR ahl ah-heh-DREHS
play golf.	*jugar al golf.* hoo-GAHR ahl gohlf
play tennis.	*jugar al tenis.* hoo-GAHR ahl TEH-nees
read.	*leer.* leh-YEHR
sew.	*coser.* koh-SEHR
ski.	*esquiar.* ehs-kee-YAHR
swim.	*nadar.* nah-DAHR
take pictures.	*sacar fotografías.* sah-KAHR foh-toh-grah-FEE-yahs
travel.	*viajar.* bee-yah-HAHR
I like baking.	*Me gusta la repostería.* meh GOOS-tah lah rreh-poh-steh-REE-yah
I like sports.	*Me gustan los deportes.* meh GOOS-tahn lohs deh-POHR-tehs

continues

Feelings

I'm ...	*Estoy* ... ehs-TOY
afraid.	*asustado(a)*. ah-soos-TAH-doh (dah)
angry.	*enojado(a)*. eh-noh-HAH-doh (dah)
anxious.	*ansioso(a)*. ahn-see-YOH-soh (sah)
ashamed.	*avergonzado(a)*. ah-behr-gohn-SAH-doh (dah)
delighted.	*encantado(a)*. ehn-kahn-TAH-doh (dah)
depressed.	*deprimido(a)*. deh-pree-MEE-doh (dah)
displeased.	*enfadado(a)*. ehn-fah-DAH-doh (dah)
flattered.	*halagado(a)*. ah-lah-GAH-doh (dah)
furious.	*furioso(a)*. foo-ree-YOH-soh (sah)
grateful.	*agradecido(a)*. ah-grah-deh-SEE-doh (dah)
happy.	*alegre*. ah-LEH-greh
irritated.	*irritado(a)*. ee-rree-TAH-doh (dah)
jealous.	*celoso(a)*. seh-LOH-soh (sah)
surprised.	*sorprendido(a)*. sohr-prehn-DEE-doh (dah)
unhappy.	*triste*. TREES-teh
worried.	*preocupado(a)*. preh-oh-koo-PAH-doh (dah)

Introductions and Family Members

I'd like to introduce you to my ...	*Me gustaría presentarle (presentarte) a mi ...* meh goos-tah-REE-yah preh-sehn-TAHR-leh (preh-sehn-TAHR-teh) ah mee ...
aunt.	*tía.* TEE-yah
boyfriend.	*novio.* NOH-bee-yoh
brother.	*hermano.* ehr-MAH-noh
brother-in-law.	*cuñado.* koo-NYAH-doh
cousin (female).	*prima.* PREE-mah
cousin (male).	*primo.* PREE-moh
daughter.	*hija.* EE-hah
daughter-in-law.	*nuera.* NWEH-rah
father.	*padre.* PAH-dreh
father-in-law.	*suegro.* SWEH-groh
girlfriend.	*novia.* NOH-bee-yah
godfather.	*padrino.* pah-DREE-noh
godmother.	*madrina.* mah-DREE-nah
granddaughter.	*nieta.* nee-YEH-tah
grandfather.	*abuelo.* ah-BWEH-loh
grandmother.	*abuela.* ah-BWEH-lah
grandson.	*nieto.* nee-YEH-toh

continues

husband.	*esposo (marido).* ehs-POH-soh (mah-REE-doh)
mother.	*madre.* MAH-dreh
mother-in-law.	*suegra.* SWEH-grah
nephew.	*sobrino.* soh-BREE-noh
niece.	*sobrina.* soh-BREE-nah
partner.	*compañero(a).* kohm-pah-NYEH-roh (rah)
significant other.	*pareja.* pah-REH-hah
sister.	*hermana.* ehr-MAH-nah
sister-in-law.	*cuñada.* koo-NYAH-dah
son.	*hijo.* EE-hoh
son-in-law.	*yerno.* YEHR-noh
stepbrother.	*hermanastro.* ehr-mah-NAHS-troh
stepfather.	*padastro.* pah-DAHS-troh
stepmother.	*madastra.* mah-DAHS-trah
stepsister.	*hermanastra.* ehr-mah-NAHS-trah
uncle.	*tío.* TEE-yoh
wife.	*esposa.* ehs-POH-sah

To express plurals, use the masculine plural form: *mis hijos* (children), *mis padres* (parents), *mis abuelos* (grandparents), *mis suegros* (in-laws), etc. Note the use of the verbs *tener*, *ser*, and *estar* to speak about the members of your family.

My father is 60 years old.	*Mi padre tiene sesenta años.* mee PAH-dreh tee-YEH-neh seh-SEHN-tah AH-nyohs
He's Italian.	*Él es italiano.* ehl ehs ee-tahl-YAH-noh
He's not sad.	*Él no está triste.* ehl noh ehs-TAH TREES-teh
My mother is 50 years old.	*Mi madre tiene cincuenta años.* mee MAH-dreh tee-YEH-neh seen-KWEHN-tah ah-NYOHS
My mother is Spanish.	*Mi madre es española.* mee MAH-dreh ehs ehs-pah-NYOH-lah
She's retired.	*Ella está jubilada.* EH-yah ehs-TAH hoo-bee-LAH-dah
My grandparents have five children.	*Mis abuelos tienen cinco hijos.* mees ah-BWEH-lohs tee-YEH-nehn SEEN-koh EE-hohs
They're nice.	*Ellos son simpáticos.* EH-yohs sohn seem-PAH-tee-kohs
They're happy.	*Ellos están alegres.* EH-yohs ehs-TAHN ah-LEH-grehs

Social Media

May I email (text) you?	*¿Puedo enviarte un correo electrónico (un mensaje de texto)?* PWEH-doh ehn-bee-YAHR-teh oon koh-RREH-yoh eh-lehk-TROH-nee-koh (oon mehn-SAH-heh deh TEHKS-toh)
What's your email address?	*¿Cuál es tu dirrección de correo electrónico?* kwahl ehs too dee-rehk-see-YOHN deh koh-RREH-yoh eh-lehk-TROH-nee-koh
What's your cell phone number?	*¿Cuál es tu número de celular (móvil)?* kwahl ehs too NOO-meh-roh deh seh-loo-LAHR (MOH-beel)
I'm on Facebook (Twitter, Instagram).	*Tengo Facebook (Twitter, Instagram).* TEHN-goh Facebook (Twitter, Instagram)
Follow me on Facebook (Twitter, Instagram).	*Sígueme en Facebook (Twitter, Instagram).* SEE-geh-meh ehn Facebook (Twitter, Instagram)
I'll follow you.	*Te sigo.* teh SEE-goh
I'd like to friend you on Facebook.	*Me gustaría enviarte una solicitud de amistad.* meh goos-tah-REE-yah ehn-bee-YAHR-teh OO-nah soh-lee-see-TOOD deh ah-mees-TAHD
Are you going to accept it?	*¿La aceptas?* lah ah-SEHP-tahs
Go to my Facebook page.	*Anda a mi página de Facebook.* AHN-dah ah mee PAH-hee-nah deh Facebook
Look at my profile page.	*Mira mi página de perfil.* MEE-rah mee PAH-hee-nah deh pehr-FEEL

I post (share) my pictures on Facebook (Instagram).	*Publico (Comparto) mis fotos en Facebook (Instagram).* POO-blee-koh (kohm-PAHR-toh) mees FOH-tohs en Facebook (Instagram)
Can I post your picture on Facebook (Instagram)?	*¿Puedo publicar tu foto en Facebook (Instagram)?* PWEH-doh poo-blee-KAHR too FOH-toh en Facebook (Instagram)?
I read your post (yours).	*Leí tu publicación (la tuya).* leh-YEE too poob-lee-kah-see-YOHN (lah TOO-yah)
Did you read my post (mine)?	*Leíste mi publicación (la mía)?* lee-YEES-teh mee poob-lee-kah-see-YOHN (lah MEE-yah)
I (don't) tweet.	*(No) Escribo en Twitter.* (noh) ehs-KREE-boh ehn Twitter
Look at my photos and videos.	*Mira mis fotos y mis videos.* MEE-rah mees FOH-tohs ee mees BEE-deh-yohs
Thank you for following me.	*Gracias por seguirme.* GRAH-see-yahs pohr seh-GEER-meh
Send me a message.	*Envíame un mensaje.* ehn-BEE-yah-meh oon mehn-SAH-heh
Would you like to chat?	*¿Te gustaría chatear?* teh goos-tah-REE-yah chah-teh-YAHR
FaceTime (Skype) me.	*Llámame por FaceTime (Skype).* YAH-mah-meh pohr FaceTime (Skype)
Do you want to go out with me?	*¿Quieres salir conmigo?* kee-YEH-rehs sah-LEER kohn-MEE-goh
What's your contact information?	*¿Cuáles son tus datos?* KWAH-lehs sohn toos DAH-tohs

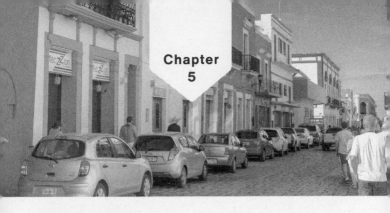

Travel

If you're taking a trip to or in a Spanish-speaking
country, the following lists of phrases will help you
get the information you need for air, bus, subway,
train, taxi, and car travel.

Air Travel

Here are some helpful phrases for traveling by air.

At Security

Here's my boarding pass and my passport.	*Aquí están mi tarjeta de embarque y mi pasaporte.* ah-KEE ehs-TAHN mee tahr-HEH-tah deh ehm-BAHR-keh ee mee pah-sah-POHR-teh
Do I have to remove my shoes (coat, belt)?	*¿Tengo que quitarme los zapatos (el abrigo, el cinturón)?* TEHN-goh keh kee-TAHR-meh lohs sah-PAH-tohs (ehl ah-BREE-goh, ehl seen-too-RROHN)
Do I have to open my suitcase (backpack)?	*¿Tengo que abrir mi maleta (mochila)?* TEHN-goh keh ah-BREER mee mah-LEH-tah (moh-CHEE-lah)
I have a medical condition. Here's a note (prescription) from my doctor.	*Tengo una condición médica. Aquí tiene una nota (receta) de mi médico.* TEHN-goh OO-nah OO-nah kohn-dee-see-YOHN MEH-dee-kah ah-KEE tee-YEH-neh OO-nah NOH-tah (rreh-SEH-tah) deh mee MEH-dee-koh

At the Travel Desk

When is there a flight to … ?	*¿Cuándo hay un vuelo a … ?* KWAHN-doh ahy oon BWEH-loh ah
Is it a direct flight?	*¿Es un vuelo directo?* ehs oon BWEH-loh dee-REHK-toh
Is there a stopover? Where?	*¿Hay escala? ¿Dónde?* ahy ehs-KAH-lah DOHN-deh

How long is the stopover?	*¿Cuánto tiempo dura la escala?* KWAHN-toh tee-YEHM-poh doo-RAH lah ehs-KAH-lah
I'd like a ... ticket.	*Quiero un billete ...* kee-YEH-roh oon bee-YEH-teh
round-trip	*de ida y vuelta* deh EE-dah ee BWEHL-tah
one-way	*de ida* deh EE-dah
tourist class	*en clase turista* ehn KLAH-seh too-REES-tah
first class	*en primera clase* ehn pree-MEH-rah KLAH-seh
business class	*en clase de negocios* ehn KLAH-seh deh neh-GOH-see-yohs
children's	*tarifa para niños* tah-REE-fah PAH-rah NEE-nyohs
student's	*tarifa para estudiantes* tah-REE-fah PAH-rah ehs-too-dee-YAHN-tehs
senior	*tarifa para jubilados (mayores)* tah-REE-fah PAH-rah hoo-bee-LAH-dohs (mah-YOH-rehs)
I'd like a seat next to the window.	*Me gustaría un asiento junto a la ventana.* meh goos-tah-REE-yah oon ah-see-YEHN-toh HOON-toh ah lah behn-TAH-nah
I'd like a seat on the aisle.	*Me gustaría un asiento de pasillo.* meh goos-tah-REE-yah oon ah-see-YEHN-toh deh pah-SEE-yoh

continues

I need more leg room.	*Necesito más espacio para las piernas.* neh-seh-SEE-toh mahs ehs-PAH-see-yoh PAH-rah lahs PYEHR-nahs
What's the fare?	*¿Cuál es la tarifa?* kwahl ehs lah tah-REE-fah
What's the flight number?	*¿Cuál es el número del vuelo?* kwahl ehs ehl NOO-meh-roh dehl BWEH-loh
When does the flight leave (arrive)?	*¿Cuándo sale (llega) el vuelo?* KWAHN-doh SAH-leh (YEH-gah) ehl BWEH-loh
From what gate do we leave?	*¿De qué puerta salimos?* deh keh PWEHR-tah sah-LEE-mohs
How long is the flight?	*¿Cuánto tiempo dura el vuelo?* KWAHN-toh tee-YEHM-poh DOO-rah ehl BWEH-loh
Are meals (snacks) (drinks) served?	*¿Se sirven comidas (bocados) (bebidas)?* seh SEER-behn KOH-mee-dahs (boh-KAH-dohs) (beh-BEE-dahs)
Is it going to leave (arrive) on time (late)?	*¿Va a salir (llegar) puntual (con retraso)?* bah ah sah-LEER (yeh-GAHR) poon-TWAHL (kohn rreh-TRAH-soh)
I have only carry-on baggage.	*Tengo solo equipaje de mano.* TEHN-goh SOH-loh eh-kee-PAH-heh deh MAH-noh
I'd like to check my bags.	*Me gustaría facturar mis maletas.* meh goos-tah-REE-yah fahk-too-RAHR mees mah-LEH-tahs
Where do I check them?	*¿Dónde puedo facturarlas?* DOHN-deh PWEH-doh fahk-too-RAHR-lahs
How much is it per bag?	*¿Cuánto cobra por maleta?* KWAHN-toh KOH-brah pohr mah-LEH-tah

On the Plane

Where's the … ?	¿Dónde está … ? DOHN-deh ehs-TAH
bathroom	*el servicio* ehl sehr-BEE-see-yoh
emergency exit	*la salida de emergencia* lah sah-LEE-dah deh eh- mehr-HEHN-see-yah
exit	*la salida* lah sah-LEE-dah
life vest	*el chaleco salvavidas* ehl chah-LEH-koh sahl- bah-BEE-dahs
oxygen mask	*la máscara de oxígeno* lah MAHS-kah-rah deh ohk-SEE-heh-noh
seatbelt	*el cinturón de seguridad* ehl seen-too-ROHN deh seh-goo-ree-DAHD

Arrival

Where's the baggage claim area?	¿Dónde está el área de reclamo de equipaje? DOHN-deh ehs-TAH ehl AH-reh-yah deh rreh-KLAH- moh deh eh-kee-PAH-heh
Where can I get a baggage cart?	¿Dónde puedo conseguir un carrito de equipaje? DOHN-deh PWEH-doh kohn- seh-GEER oon kah-RREE-toh deh eh-kee-PAH-heh
I'm looking for a porter.	*Busco a un botones.* BOOS-koh ah oon boh-TOH- nehs
Where are the elevators?	¿Dónde están los ascensores? DOHN-deh ehs-TAHN lohs ah- sehn-SOH-rehs

continues

Where's the ground transportation?	*¿Dónde están los transportes públicos?* DOHN-deh ehs-TAHN lohs trahns-POHR-tehs POOB-lee-kohs
Where are the escalators?	*¿Dónde están las escaleras mecánicas?* DOHN-deh ehs-TAHN lahs ehs-kah-LEH-rahs meh-KAH-nee-kahs
Where's the car rental?	*¿Dónde está el alquiler de coches?* DOHN-deh ehs-TAH ehl ahl-kee-LEHR deh KOH-chehs
Where's customs?	*¿Dónde está la aduana?* DOHN-deh ehs-TAH lah ah-DWAH-nah
Where can I get a … ?	*¿Dónde puedo tomar un … ?* DOHN-deh PWEH-doh toh-MAHR oon
bus	*autobús* ow-toh-BOOS
rideshare	*vehículo compartido* beh-HEE-koo-loh kohm-pahr-TEE-doh
subway	*metro* MEH-troh
taxi	*taxi* TAHK-see
train	*tren* trehn
Where can I change my money?	*¿Dónde puedo cambiar mi dinero?* DOHN-deh PWEH-doh kahm-bee-YAHR mee dee-NEH-roh
My suitcase is damaged.	*Mi maleta está dañada.* mee mah-LEH-tah ehs-TAH dah-NYAH-dah
I can't find my bag(s).	*No puedo encontrar mi(s) maleta(s).* noh PWEH-doh ehn-kohn-TRAHR mee(s) mah-LEH-tah(s)
What should I do?	*¿Qué tengo que hacer?* keh TEHN-goh keh ah-SEHR

| Where should I go? | ¿Adónde debería ir?
ah-DOHN-deh deh-beh-REE-yah eer |

At Customs

I'm staying at the ... hotel.	Me quedo en el hotel ... . meh KEH-doh ehn ehl oh-TEHL
I'm staying here ...	Me quedo aquí ... meh KEH-doh ah-KEE
... days.	... días. DEE-yahs
a week.	una semana. OO-nah seh-MAH-nah
two weeks.	dos semanas. dohs seh-MAH-nahs
a month.	un mes. oon mehs
I'm on vacation.	Estoy de vacaciones. ehs-TOY deh bah-kah-see-YOH-nehs
I'm visiting family.	Visito a mi familia. bee-SEE-toh ah mee fah-MEE-lyah
I'm on a business trip.	Estoy en un viaje de negocios. ehs-TOY ehn oon bee-YAH-heh deh neh-GOH-see-yohs
Here's ...	Aquí está ... ah-KEE ehs-TAH
my custom declaration form.	mi formulario de declaración aduanera. mee fohr-moo-LAH-ree-yoh deh deh-klah-rah-see-YOHN ah-dwah-NEH-rah
my passport.	mi pasaporte. mee pah-sah-POHR-teh
my driver's license.	mi licencia de conducer. mee lee-SEHN-see-yah deh kohn-doo-SEER

continues

I've nothing to declare.

No tengo nada que declarar.
noh TEHN-goh NAH-dah keh
deh-klah-RAHR

Boat Travel

At what time does the boat leave the port?

¿A qué hora sale el barco del puerto?
ah keh OH-rah SAH-leh ehl
BAHR-koh dehl PWEHR-toh

What's the next port?

¿Cuál es el próximo puerto?
kwahl ehs ehl PROHK-see-moh
PWEHR-toh

How long does the crossing take?

¿Cuánto tiempo dura la travesía?
KWAHN-toh tee-YEHM-poh
DOO-rah lah trah-beh-SEE-yah

How long will we remain in port?

¿Cuánto tiempo permaneceremos en el puerto?
KWAHN-toh tee-YEHM-poh
pehr-mah-neh-seh-REH-mohs
ehn ehl PWEHR-toh

At what time do we have to be back on board?

¿A qué hora tenemos que volver a bordo?
ah keh OH-rah teh-NEH-mohs
keh bohl-BEHR ah BOHR-doh

What do you have for seasickness?

¿Qué tiene para el mareo?
keh tee-YEH-neh PAH-rah ehl
mah-REH-yoh

At what time do we arrive in port?

¿A qué hora llegamos al puerto?
ah keh OH-rah yeh-GAH-mohs
ahl PWEHR-toh

Bus Travel

Where's the nearest bus stop?

¿Dónde está la parada de autobús más cercana?
DOHN-deh ehs-TAH lah pah-
RAH-dah deh ow-toh-BOOS
mahs sehr-KAH-nah

Is this the bus that goes to … ?	*¿Éste es el autobús que va a … ?* EHS-teh ehs ehl ow-toh-BOOS keh bah ah
How much is the fare?	*¿Cuánto cuesta el billete?* KWAHN-toh KWEHS-tah ehl bee-YEH-teh
Do I need exact change?	*¿Necesito cambio exacto?* neh-seh-SEE-toh KAHM-bee-yoh ehk-SAHK-toh

Subway Travel

Where's the nearest subway?	*¿Dónde está la estación de metro más cercana?* DOHN-deh ehs-TAH lah ehs-tah-see-YOHN deh MEH-troh mahs sehr-KAH-nah
Where can I buy a ticket?	*¿Dónde puedo comprar un billete?* DOHN-deh PWEH-doh kohm-PRAHR oon bee-YEH-teh
How much is the fare?	*¿Cuánto es la tarifa?* KWAHN-toh ehs lah tah-REE-fah
Where can I find a map?	*¿Dónde hay un mapa?* DOHN-deh ahy oon MAH-pah
How many more stops are there?	*¿Hay cuántas paradas más?* ahy KWAHN-tahs pah-RAH-dahs mahs
What's the next station?	*¿Cuál es la prómixa estación?* kwahl ehs lah PROHK-see-mah ehs-tah-see-YOHN
Should I get off here?	*¿Debo bajar aquí?* DEH-boh bah-HAHR ah-KEE

Travel by Taxi/Rideshare

Travel by taxi and rideshare is increasingly popular.
Tipping varies from country to country, so it's best
to find out the right thing to do at an airport
information desk or from the concierge at your
hotel. When in doubt, if you're pleased with the
service, consider rewarding your driver.

Where's the nearest taxi stand?	*¿Dónde está la parada de taxi más cercana?* DOHN-deh ehs-TAH lah pah-RAH-dah deh TAHK-see mahs sehr-KAH-nah
Would you please call me a cab?	*¿Puede conseguirme un taxi por favor?* PWEH-deh kohn-seh-GEER-meh oon TAHK-see pohr fah-BOHR
I want to go to ...	*Quiero ir a (al, a la) ... .* kee-YEH-roh eer ah (ahl, ah lah)
How much is it to go to ... ?	*¿Cuánto cuesta ir a (al, a la) ... ?* KWAHN-toh KWEHS-tah eer ah (ahl, ah lah)...
Stop here please.	*Pare aquí por favor.* PAH-reh ah-KEE pohr fah-BOHR
Wait for me please.	*Espéreme por favor.* ehs-PEH-reh-meh pohr fah-BOHR
How much do I owe you?	*¿Cuánto le debo?* KWAHN-toh leh DEH-boh

Train Travel

Where's the nearest train station?	*¿Dónde está la estación de tren más cercana?* DOHN-deh ehs-TAH lah ehs-tah-see-YOHN deh trehn mahs sehr-KAH-nah

I'd like a ...	*Me gustaría ...*
	meh goos-tah-REE-yah
first- (second-) class ticket.	*un billete de primera (segunda) clase.*
	oon bee-YEH-teh deh pree-MEH-rah (seh-GOON-dah) KLAH-seh
round-trip ticket.	*un billete de ida y vuelta.*
	oon bee-YEH-teh deh EE-dah ee BWEHL-tah
Is it a local (express)?	*¿Es un tren local (un rápido)?*
	ehs oon trehn loh-KAHL (oon RRAH-pee-doh)
From what platform does it leave?	*¿De qué andén sale?*
	deh keh ahn-DEHN SAH-leh

Car Travel

I'd like to rent ...	*Me gustaría alquilar ...*
	meh goos-tah-REE-yah ahl-kee-LAHR
a car.	*un coche.*
	oon KOH-cheh
a 4-wheel drive.	*un cuatro por cuatro.*
	oon KWAH-troh pohr KWAH-troh
a minivan.	*un minivan.*
	oon mee-nee-BAHN
an SUV.	*un VUD.*
	oon beh-oo-DEH
an RV.	*una caravana.*
	OO-nah kah-rah-BAH-nah
How much does it cost per day (per week) (per kilometer)?	*¿Cuánto cuesta por día (por semana) (por kilómetro)?*
	KWAHN-toh KWEHS-tah pohr DEE-yah (pohr seh-MAH-nah) (por kee-LOH-meh-troh)

continues

Can I get unlimited mileage?	*Puedo obtener kilometraje ilimitado?* PWEH-doh ohb-teh-NEHR kee-loh-meh-TRAH-heh ee-lee-mee-TAH-doh
Does the car have … ?	*¿El coche tiene … ?* ehl KOH-cheh tee-YEH-neh
ABS	*sistema de frenado (ABS)* sees-TEH-mah deh freh-NAH-doh (ah-beh-EHS)
automatic transmission	*transmisión automática* trahns-mee-see-YOHN ow-toh-MAH-tee-kah
Bluetooth	*Bluetooth* BLOO-tooth
GPS	*GPS* heh-peh-EH-seh
manual transmission	*transmisión manual* trahns-mee-see-YOHN mah-NWAHL
power steering	*dirección asistida* dee-rehk-see-YOHN ah-sees-TEE-dah
power windows	*ventanillas eléctricas* behn-tah-NEE-yahs eh-LEHK-tree-kahs
How much is the insurance?	*¿Cuánto es el seguro?* KWAHN-toh ehs ehl seh-GOO-roh
Is the gas included?	*¿Está incluída la gasolina?* ehs-TAH een-kloo-WEE-dah lah gah-soh-LEE-nah
What kind of gas does it take?	*¿Qué tipo de gasolina utiliza?* keh TEE-poh deh gah-soh-LEE-nah oo-tee-LEE-sah
What's the speed limit?	*¿Cuál es el límite de velocidad?* kwahl ehs ehl LEE-mee-teh deh beh-loh-see-DAHD
Do you sell maps?	*¿Vende mapas?* BEHN-deh MAH-pahs

| Do you accept credit cards? Which ones? | *¿Acepta tarjetas de crédito? ¿Cuáles?*
ah-SEHP-tah tahr-HEH-tahs deh KREH-dee-toh KWAH-lehs |

When you rent a car in a foreign country, make sure it has a jack (*un gato* [oon GAH-toh]) and a spare tire (*una goma de repuesto* [OO-nah GOH-mah deh rreh-PWEHS-toh]).

Distance is measured in kilometers. One kilometer is the equivalent of .62 miles.

Car Problems

My car broke down.	*Mi auto se averió.* mee OW-toh seh ah-beh-ree-YOH
Where's the nearest gas station?	*¿Dónde está la gasolinera la más cercana?* DOHN-deh ehs-TAH lah gah-soh-lee-NEH-rah lah mahs sehr-KAH-nah
I have a flat tire.	*Tengo una llanta pinchada.* TEHN-goh OO-nah YAHN-tah peen-CHAH-dah
The battery died.	*La batería se descargó.* lah bah-teh-ree-YAH seh dehs-kahr-GOH
The car won't start.	*El auto no arranca.* ehl OW-toh noh ah-RRAHN-kah
The car is overheating.	*El auto se sobrecalienta.* ehl OW-toh seh soh-breh-kah-lee-YEHN-tah
Water is leaking from the radiator.	*El agua está goteando del radiador.* ehl AH-gwah ehs-TAH goh-teh-YAHN-doh dehl rrah-dee-yah-DOHR

continues

Oil is leaking from the engine.	*El aceite está goteando del motor.* ehl ah-SEHY-teh ehs-TAH goh-teh-YAHN-doh dehl moh-TOHR
I locked the keys inside the car.	*Cerré las llaves dentro del auto.* seh-RREH lahs YAH-behs DEHN-troh dehl OW-toh
I've had an accident.	*Tuve un accidente.* TOO-beh oon ahk-see-DEHN-teh
Can you help me?	*¿Puede ayudarme?* PWEH-deh ah-yoo-DAHR-meh
Can you tow (fix) my car?	*¿Puede remolcar (reparar) mi auto?* PWEH-deh rreh-mohl-KAHR (rreh-pah-RAHR) mee OW-toh
How long will it take?	*¿Cuánto tiempo tardará?* KWAHN-toh tee-YEHM-poh tahr-dah-RAH
When will it be ready?	*¿Cuándo estará listo?* KWAHN-doh ehs-tah-RAH LEES-toh
How much do I owe you?	*¿Cuánto le debo?* KWAHN-toh leh DEH-boh

Getting Directions

Continue ...	*Continúe ...* kohn-tee-NOO-weh
Cross ...	*Cruce ...* KROO-seh
Follow ...	*Siga ...* SEE-gah
Go down ...	*Baje ...* BAH-heh
Go up ...	*Suba ...* SOO-bah
Go ...	*Vaya ...* BAH-yah
Pass ...	*Pase ...* PAH-seh

Take …	*Tome* … TOH-meh
Turn …	*Doble* … DOH-bleh
Walk …	*Camine* … kah-MEE-neh
It's …	*Está* … ehs-TAH
above …	*encima de* … ehn-SEE-mah deh
at …	*a* … ah
behind …	*detrás de* … deh-TRAHS deh
far (from) …	*lejos de* … LEH-hohs deh
from …	*de* … deh
in …	*en* … ehn
in front of …	*enfrente de* … ehn-FREHN-teh deh
near (to) …	*cerca (de)* … SEHR-kah (deh)
next to …	*junto a* … HOON-toh ah
opposite …	*frente a* … FREHN-teh ah
to …	*a* … ah
toward …	*hacia* … AH-see-yah
to the north …	*al norte* … ahl NOHR-teh
to the east …	*al este* … ahl EHS-teh
to the south …	*al sur* … ahl soor
to the west …	*al oeste* … ahl oh-WEHS-teh

continues

to the right ...	*a la derecha ...* ah lah deh-REH-chah
to the left ...	*a la izquierda ...* ah lah ees-kee-YEHR-dah
It's two blocks from here.	*Está a dos cuadras de aquí.* ehs-TAH ah dohs KWAH-drahs deh ah-KEE

Note that *a + el* becomes *al* and *de + el* becomes *del*.

It's next to the theater.	*Está junto al teatro.* ehs-TAH HOON-toh ahl teh-YAH-troh
It's in front of the bank.	*Está enfrente del banco.* ehs-TAH ehn-FREHN-teh dehl BAHN-koh

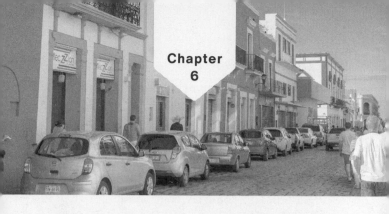

Accommodations

For some, when it comes to travel accommodations, the bare necessities are enough. Others, however, prefer downright opulence. And then there are those with needs in between the two. Whatever your personal requirements, this chapter will help you get the room and services you desire.

Helpful reminder: To be polite, use *por favor* (pohr fah-BOHR) to express "please" when asking someone to perform a service for you.

Hotel Accommodations

If you plan to stay in a Spanish-speaking country, possible accommodations include:

- *Un hotel* (oon oh-TEHL) is usually rated by the government or a travel-rating organization using a star system ranging from inexpensive (one star) to very expensive (five stars). Every hotel has an outside plaque indicating an *H* for hotel.

- *Una pensión* (OO-nah pehn-see-YOHN) is similar to a rooming house, where guests pay for a room and all or part of their meals.

- *Un albergue* (oon ahl-BEHR-geh) is a small, modest inn generally found in rural areas.

- *Los albergues juveniles* (lohs ahl-BEHR-gehs hoo-beh-NEE-lehs) are youth hostels.

- *Un parador* (oon pah-rah-DOHR) are first-class hotels run by the state. Many are former royal homes, converted castles, or monasteries.

- *Un hostal* (oon ohs-TAHL) is a small hotel or inn without a restaurant.

- *Un refugio* (oon rreh-FOO-hee-yoh) is a private retreat or lodge in the country that can be rented for a specified time period.

You can rent (*alquilar*, ahl-kee-LAHR):

- **A house:** *una casa* (OO-nah KAH-sah)

- **An apartment:** *un apartamento* (oon ah-pahr-tah-MEHN-toh)

- **A condo:** *un piso* (oon PEE-soh) [Spanish], *un departamento* (oon deh-pahr-tah-MEHN-toh) [Latin America]

- **A cabin:** *una cabaña* (OO-nah kah-BAH-nyah)

You can stay in (*quedarse en*, keh-DAHR-seh ehn):

- **A bed and breakfast:** *un alojamiento y desayuno* (oon ah-loh-hah-mee-YEHN-toh ee deh-sah-YOO-noh)

- **A campsite:** *un campamento* (oon kahm-pah-MEHN-toh)

Tipping

Hotel bills include a service charge, which can range from 10 to 15%. However, it's customary to tip the bellhop who takes care of your luggage, the housekeeper, room service, and anyone who calls for a taxi. If a concierge is present and performs special services—making restaurant reservations, procuring tickets, etc.—a tip is warranted.

Amenities, Facilities, and Services

Is (Are) there ... ?	¿Hay ... ? ahy
air-conditioning	*aire acondicionado* AHY-reh ah-kohn-dee-see-yoh-NAH-doh
babysitting services	*cuidado de niños* kwee-DAH-doh deh NEE-nyohs
a bar	*un bar* oon bahr
a bellhop	*un botones* oon boh-TOH-nehs
a beauty salon	*un salón de belleza* oon sah-LOHN de beh-YEH-sah
a bridal suite	*una suite nupcial* OO-nah SWEE-teh noop-see-YAHL
a business center	*un centro de negocios* oon SEHN-troh deh neh-GOH-see-yohs
a coffee machine	*una cafetera* OO-nah kah-feh-TEH-rah

continues

concierge service	*servicio de conserjería* sehr-BEE-see-yoh deh koh-sehr-heh-REE-yah
a crib	*una cuna* OO-nah KOO-nah
a doorman	*un portero* oon pohr-TEH-roh
dry-cleaning service	*una tintorería* OO-nah teen-toh-reh-REE-yah
an elevator	*un ascensor* oon ah-sehn-SOHR
a fitness center	*un gimnasio* oon heem-NAH-see-yoh
a gift shop	*una tienda de regalos* OO-nah tee-YEHN- dah deh rreh-GAH-lohs
handicap access	*acceso para los minusválidos* ahk-SEH-soh PAH-rah lohs mee-noos-BAH-lee-dohs
handicap facilities	*servicios para los minusválidos* sehr-BEE-see-yohs PAH-rah lohs mee-noos-BAH-lee-dohs
housekeeping	*servicio de limpieza* sehr-BEE-see-yoh deh leem-pee-YEH-sah
an ice maker	*un dispensador de hielo* oon dees-pehn-sah-DOHR deh ee-YEH-loh
Internet service	*servicio de Internet* sehr-BEE-see-yoh deh Internet
a laundry	*una lavandería* OO-nah lah-bahn-deh-REE-yah
a mini-bar	*un minibar* oon mee-nee-BAHR
pay-per-view	*televisión de pago a la carta* teh-leh-bee-see-YOHN deh PAH-goh ah lah KAHR-tah

a restaurant	*un restaurante* oon rrehs-tow-RAHN-teh
room service	*servicio de habitación* sehr-BEE-see-yoh deh ah-bee-tah-see-YOHN
a safe	*una caja fuerte* OO-nah KAH-hah FWEHR-teh
shuttle service	*servicio de traslados* sehr-BEE-see-yoh deh trahs-LAH-dohs
a sofa bed	*un sofá-cama* oon soh-FAH-KAH-mah
a spa	*un spa* oon spah
a swimming pool (indoor)	*una piscina (cubierta)* OO-nah pee-SEE-nah (koo-bee-YEHR-tah)
TV (cable)	*televisión (por cable)* teh-leh-bee-see-YOHN (pohr KAH-bleh)
valet parking	*servicio de aparcamiento* sehr-BEE-see-yoh deh ah-pahr-kah-mee-YEHN-toh
vending machines	*máquinas expendedoras* MAH-kee-nahs ehs-pehn-deh-DOH-rahs
Wi-Fi service	*servicio de WiFi* sehr-BEE-see-yoh deh Wi-Fi

Special Amenities

| At what time does the salon (spa) (fitness center) open (close)? | *¿A qué hora abre (cierra) el salón (spa) (gimnasio)?*
 ah keh OH-rah AH-breh (see-YEH-rrah) ehl sah-LOHN (spah) (heem-NAH-see-yoh) |
| I'd like an appointment for … at … o'clock … . | *Me gustaría una cita para … a la(s) … .*
 meh goos-tah-REE-yah OO-nah SEE-tah PAH-rah … ah lah(s) |

continues

a facial	*un tratamiento facial* oon trah-tah-mee-YEHN-toh fah-see-YAHL
a haircut	*un corte de pelo* oon KOHR-teh deh PEH-loh
a (French) manicure	*una manicura (francesa)* OO-nah mah-nee-KOO-rah (frahn-SEH-sah)
a massage	*un masaje* oon mah-SAH-heh
a pedicure	*una pedicura* OO-nah peh-dee-KOO-rah
a shampoo	*un champú* oon chahm-POO
a shave	*una afeitada* OO-nah ah-feh-yee-TAH-dah
a waxing	*una depilación* OO-nah deh-pee-lah-see-YOHN
Please wash and blow-dry my hair.	*Por favor láveme el pelo y séquelo con secadora.* poh fah-BOHR LAH-beh-meh ehl PEH-loh ee SEH-keh-loh con seh-kah-DOH-rah
How much does it cost?	*¿Cuánto cuesta?* KWAHN-toh KWEHS-tah
Is the tip included?	*¿Está incluida la propina?* ehs-TAH een-KLWEE-doh lah proh-PEE-nah
Is there a fee to use the gym?	*¿Hay algún cargo por usar el gimnasio?* ahy ahl-GOON KAHR-goh pohr oo-SAHR ehl heem-NAH-see-yoh
How much is it?	*¿Cuánto cuesta?* KWAHN-toh KWEHS-tah
Is there ... ?	*¿Hay ... ?* ahy
a pool	*una piscina* OO-nah pee-SEE-nah
a sauna	*una sauna* OO-nah SOW-nah

a steam room	*una sala de vapor*
	OO-nah SAH-lah deh bah-POHR
a jacuzzi	*un jacuzzi*
	oon hah-KOO-zee

Special Needs

We need special accommodations.	*Tenemos necesidades especiales de alojamiento.* teh-NEH-mohs neh-seh-see-DAH-dehs ehs-peh-see-YAH-lehs deh ah-loh-hah-mee-YEHN-toh
What services do you have for the handicapped?	*¿Qué servicios hay para los minusválidos?* keh sehr-BEE-see-yohs ahy PAH-rah lohs mee-noos-BAH-lee-dohs
Are guide (service) dogs allowed?	*¿Se permitten perros lazarillos (guías)?* seh pehr-MEE-tehn PEH-rrohs lah-sah-REE-yohs (GEE-yahs)
Are there ramps?	*¿Hay rampas?* ahy RRAHM-pahs
Are signs written in Braille?	*¿Hay letreros escritos en braille?* ahy leh-TREH-rohs ehs-KREE-tohs ehn BRAH-yeh
Can you provide a wheelchair (walker)?	*¿Podría facilitar una silla de ruedas (un andador ortopédico)?* poh-DREE-yah fah-see-lee-TAHR OO-nah SEE-yah deh RRWEH-dahs (oon ahn-dah-DOHR ohr-toh-PEH-dee-koh)
Is there a doctor (dentist) available?	*¿Hay un doctor (un dentista) a nuestra disposición?* ahy oon DOHK-tohr (oon dehn-TEES-tah) ah NWEHS-trah dees-poh-see-see-YOHN

continues

Is there a ground floor (first floor) room available?	*¿Hay una habitación en la planta baja?* ahy OO-nah ah-bee-tah-see-YOHN ehn lah PLAHN-tah BAH-hah
Are there toilet facilities for the handicapped?	*¿Hay dispositivos de asistencia para minusválidos en los baños?* ahy dees-poh-see-TEE-bohs deh ah-sees-TEHN-see-yah PAH-rah mee-noos-BAH-lee-dohs ehn lohs BAH-nyohs
Are there bathrooms on the ground floor?	*¿Hay baños en la planta baja?* ahy BAH-nyohs ehn lah PLAHN-tah BAH-hah
Are there bars in the bathroom (shower)?	*¿Hay barras en los baños (en la ducha)?* ahy BAH-rrahs ehn lohs BAH-nyohs (ehn lah DOO-chah)
Is there a refrigerator (freezer) in the room?	*¿Hay un refrigerador (un congelador) en la habitación?* ahy oon rreh-free-heh-rah-DOHR (oon kohn-heh-lah-DOHR) ehn lah ah-bee-tah-see-YOHN
Do you have close-captioned TV?	*¿Tiene televisiones con subtítulos?* tee-YEH-neh teh-lee-bee-see-YOH-nehs kohn soob-TEE-too-lohs
Is there handicapped parking?	*¿Hay estacionamiento para los minusválidos?* ahy ehs-tah-see-yoh-nah mee-YEHN-toh PAH-rah lohs mee-noos-BAH-lee-dohs
Where can I get a handicapped parking permit?	*¿Dónde puedo conseguir una licencia de estacionamiento para minusválidos?* DOHN-deh PWEH-doh kohn-see-GEER OO-nah lee-SEHN see-yah deh ehs-tah-see-yoh-nah-mee-YEHN-toh PAH-rah mee-noos-BAH-lee-dohs

Where can I find a compound pharmacy?	*¿Dónde hay una farmacia haciendo preparaciones magistrales?* DOHN-deh ahy OO-nah fahr-MAH-see-yah ah-see-YEHN-doh preh-pah-rah-see-YOH-nehs mah-hee-STRAH-lehs
Where's an all-night pharmacy?	*¿Dónde hay una farmacia de guardia?* DOHN-deh ahy OO-nah fahr-MAH-see-yah deh GWAHR-dee-yah
Where can I buy hearing aid batteries?	*¿Dónde puedo comprar pilas para audífonos?* DOHN-deh PWEH-doh kohm-PRAHR PEE-lahs PAH-rah ow-DEE-foh-nohs
Does anyone know American Sign Language?	*¿Alguien sabe lenguaje de señas americano?* AHL-gee-yehn SAH-beh lehn-GWAH-heh deh SEH-nyahs ah-meh-ree-KAH-noh

Checking In

I (don't) have a reservation.	*(No) Tengo reservación.* (noh) TEHN-goh rreh-sehr-bah-see-YOHN
Are there any available rooms?	*Hay habitaciones disponibles?* ahy ah-bee-tah-see-YOH-nehs dees-poh-NEE-blehs
I'd like ...	*Me gustaría ...* mee goos-tah-REE-yah ...
a double (single) room.	*una habitación con dos camas (una sola cama).* OO-nah ah-bee-tah-see-YOHN kohn dohs KAH-mahs (OO-nah SOH-lah KAH-mah)
adjoining rooms.	*habitaciones contiguas.* ah-bee-tah-see-YOH-nehs kohn-TEE-gwahs

continues

a non-adjoining room.	*una habitación no contingua a otra.* OO-nah ah-bee-tah-see-YOHN noh kohn-TEE-gwah ah OH-trah
I'd like a room (an apartment) ...	*Me gustaría una habitación (un apartamento) ...* meh goos-tah-REE-yah OO-nah ah-bee-tah-see-YOHN (oon ah-pahr-tah-MEHN-toh)
facing the courtyard.	*que dé al patio.* keh deh ahl PAH-tee-yoh
facing the garden.	*con vista al jardín.* kohn BEES-tah ahl hahr-DEEN
facing the ocean.	*con vista al mar.* kohn BEES-tah ahl mahr
facing the street.	*que dé a la calle.* keh deh ah lah KAH-yeh
on the ground floor.	*en la planta baja.* ehn lah PLAHN-tah BAH-hah
that's handicap accessible.	*con acceso a los minusválidos.* kohn ahk-SEH-soh ah lohs mee-noos-BAH-lee-dohs
with a balcony.	*con balcón.* kohn bahl-KOHN
How much is it per night? (week) (month)	*¿Cuánto cuesta por noche? (semana) (mes)* KWAHN-toh KWEHS-tah pohr NOH-cheh (seh-MAH-nah) (mehs)
I (we) will be staying one night (a week, two weeks).	*Voy a quedarme (nos) una noche (una semana, dos semanas)* boy ah keh-DAHR-meh (nohs) OO-nah NOH-cheh (OO-nah seh-MAH-nah, dohs seh-MAH-nahs)
How much do you charge for children?	*¿Cuánto cobra por los niños?* KWAN-toh KOH-brah pohr lohs NEE-nyohs

Could you put a crib (another bed) in the room?	*¿Podría poner una cuna (otra cama) en la habitación?* poh-DREE-yah POH-nehr OO-nah KOO-nah (OH-trah KAH-mah) ehn lah ah-bee-tah-see-YOHN
Is there a discount for seniors (children)?	*¿Hay un descuento para los mayores (los niños)?* ahy oon dehs-KWEHN-toh PAH-rah lohs mah-YOH-rehs (lohs NEE-nyohs)
Is there a charge for the Internet (WiFi)?	*¿Cuánto cobra para el servicio de Internet (WiFi)?* KWAHN-toh KOH-brah PAH-rah ehl sehr-BEE-see-yoh deh Internet (WiFi)
Is breakfast included?	*¿Está incuido el desayuno?* ehs-TAH een-KLWEE-doh ehl deh-sah-YOO-noh
What floor is it on?	*¿En qué piso está?* ehn keh PEE-soh ehs-TAH
What's the room number?	*¿Cuál es el número de la habitación?* kwahl ehs ehl NOO-meh-roh deh lah ah-bee-tah-see-YOHN
May I see the room?	*¿Podría ver la habitación?* poh-DREE-yah behr lah ah-bee-tah-see-YOHN
Is everything included?	*¿Está incluido todo?* ehs-TAH een-KLWEE-doh TOH-doh
I (don't) like it.	*(No) Me gusta.* (noh) meh GOOS-tah
May I see another room?	*Podría ver otra habitación?* poh-DREE-yah behr OH-trah ah-bee-tah-see-YOHN
Is there something … ?	*¿Hay algo … ?* ahy AHL-goh
better	*mejor* meh-HOHR

continues

bigger	*más grande* mahs GRAHN-deh
smaller	*más pequeño* mahs peh-KEH-nyoh
cheaper	*más barato* mahs bah-RAH-toh
quieter	*más privado* mahs pree-BAH-doh
May I please have the key?	*¿Puedo obtener la llave por favor?* PWEH-doh ohb-teh-NEHR lah YAH-beh pohr fah-BOHR
Where's the elevator?	*¿Dónde está el ascensor?* DOHN-deh ehs-TAH ehl ah-sehn-SOHR
Where are the emergency exits?	*¿Dónde están las salidas de emergencia?* DOHN-deh ehs-TAHN lahs sah-LEE-dahs deh eh-mehr-HEHN-see-yah
Can somebody help me with my luggage?	*¿Alguien puede ayudarme con mis maletas?* AHL-gee-yehn PWEH-deh ah-yoo-DAHR-meh kohn mees mah-LEH-tahs
At what time do I have to check out?	*¿A qué hora debo dejar la habitación?* ah keh OH-rah DEH-boh deh-HAHR lah ah-bee-tah-see-YOHN
Is there automatic checkout?	*¿Hay salida automática?* ahy sah-LEE-dah ow-toh-MAH-tee-kah

Room Needs

I need ...	*Necesito ...* neh-seh-SEE-toh
an adaptor.	*un adaptador.* oon ah-dahp-tah-DOHR
an ashtray.	*un cenicero.* oon seh-nee-SEH-roh

a bar of soap.	*una pastilla de jabón.* OO-nah pahs-TEE-yah deh hah-BOHN
a blanket.	*una manta.* OO-nah MAHN-tah
clean sheets.	*sábanas limpias.* SAH-bah-nahs LEEM-pee-yahs
conditioner (hair).	*suavisante.* swah-bee-SAHN-teh
a hair dryer.	*un secador de pelo.* oon seh-kah-DOHR deh PEH-loh
hangers.	*unas perchas.* OO-nahs PEHR-chahs
ice cubes.	*cubitos de hielo.* koo-BEE-tohs deh YEH-loh
a key.	*una llave.* OO-nah YAH-beh
mineral water.	*agua mineral.* AH-gwah mee-neh-RAHL
mouthwash.	*enjuage bucal.* ehn-HWAH-geh boo-KAHL
a pillow.	*una almohada.* OO-nah ahl-moh-AH-dah
shampoo.	*champú.* chahm-POO
a shower cap.	*un gorro de ducha.* oon GOH-rroh deh DOO-chah
tissues.	*pañuelos de papel.* pah-nyoo-WEH-lohs deh pah-PEHL
toilet paper.	*papel higiénico.* pah-PEHL ee-hee-YEH-nee-koh
towels.	*toallas.* toh-WAH-yahs
a transformer.	*un transformador.* oon trahns-fohr-mah-DOHR

Breakfast

Where's the dining room?	*¿Dónde está el comedor?* DOHN-deh ehs-TAH ehl koh-meh-DOHR
Is there a buffet?	*¿Hay un bufé?* ahy oon boo-FEH
What's the number for room service?	*¿Cuál es el número para el servicio en habitación?* kwahl ehs ehl NOO-meh-roh PAH-rah ehl sehr-BEE-see-yoh ehn ah-bee-tah-see-YOHN
I'd (We'd) like …	*Me (Nos) gustaría(n) …* meh (nohs) goos-tah-ree-yah(n)
bacon.	*tocino.* toh-SEE-noh
bread.	*pan.* pahn
butter.	*mantequilla.* mahn-teh-KEE-yah
cereal.	*cereal.* seh-reh-YAHL
cocoa.	*cocoa.* [Latin America] koh-KOH-wah
coffee (decaffeinated) (black).	*café (descafeinado) (solo) (negro).* kah-FEH (dehs-kah-feh-yee-NAH-doh) (SOH-loh) (NEH-groh)
cold cuts.	*fiambres.* fee-YAHM-brehs
cream.	*crema.* KREH-mah
eggs.	*huevos.* WEH-bohs
fried	*fritos* FREE-tohs
hard-boiled	*duros* DOO-rohs
poached	*escalfados* ehs-kahl-FAH-dohs

scrambled	*revueltos* rreh-BWEHL-tohs
soft-boiled	*pasados por agua* pah-SAH-dohs pohr AH-gwah
French toast.	*pan francés.* pahn frahn-SEHS
fresh fruit.	*fruta fresca.* FROO-tah FREHS-kah
hot chocolate.	*chocolate.* choh-koh-LAH-teh
jam.	*mermelada.* mehr-meh-LAH-dah
juice.	*jugo de ...* [Latin America], *zumo de ...* [Spain] HOO-goh deh, SOO-moh deh
apple	*manzana* mahn-SAH-nah
grape	*uva* OO-bah
grapefruit	*pomelo* poh-MEH-loh
orange	*naranja* nah-RAHN-hah
pineapple	*piña* PEE-nyah
lemon.	*limón.* lee-MOHN
margarine.	*margarina.* mahr-gah-REE-nah
milk.	*leche.* LEH-cheh
mineral water (flat) (bubbly).	*agua mineral (sin gas)* *(con gas).* AH-gwah mee-neh-RAHL (seen gahs) (kohn gahs)
oatmeal.	*avena.* ah-BEH-nah

continues

an omelet.	*una tortilla francesa (una tortilla de huevo* [Mexico]). OO-nah tohr-TEE-yah frahn-SEH-sah (OO-nah tohr-TEE-yah deh HWEH-boh)
pancakes.	*panqueques* [Latin America]. pahn-KEH-kehs
pastries.	*pan dulce.* pahn DOOL-seh
rolls.	*panecillos.* pah-neh-SEE-yohs
sausages.	*salchichas.* sahl-CHEE-chahs
sugar.	*azúcar.* ah-SOO-kahr
tea (decaffeinated).	*té (descafeinado).* teh (dehs-kah-feh-yee-NAH-doh)
toast.	*pan tostado.* pahn tohs-TAH-doh

Child Care

Give him (her) breakfast (lunch) (dinner).	*Dale el desayuno (el almuerzo) (la cena).* DAH-leh ehl deh-sah-YOO-noo (ehl ahl-MWEHR-soh) (lah SEH-nah)
Feed him/her (them) at ... o'clock.	*Dale(les) de comer a la(s) ...* DAH-lehs deh koh-MEHR ah lah(s)
He (She) doesn't eat ...	*No come ...* noh KOH-meh
Bathe him (her) at ... o'clock (in the morning, evening).	*Dale un baño a la(s) ... (de la mañana, de la noche).* DAH-leh oon BAH-nyoh ah lah(s) ... (deh lah mah-NYAH-nah, deh lah NOH-cheh)

He (She) prefers a shower.	*Prefiere una ducha.* preh-fee-YEH-reh OO-nah DOO-chah
Don't allow the children to …	*No permitas que los niños …* noh pehr-MEE-tahs keh lohs NEE-nyohs
eat sweets.	*coman dulces.* KOH-mahn DOOL-sehs
drink soda.	*beban refrescos.* BEH-bahn rreh-FREHS-kohs
talk too long on their cell phone.	*hablen mucho por su celular (móvil [Spain]).* AH-blehn MOO-choh pohr soo seh-loo-LAHR, MOH-beel
watch TV.	*miren la televisión.* MEE-rehn lah teh-leh-bee-see-YOHN
Limit screen time to … minutes.	*Limita el tiempo de pantalla ah … minutos.* lee-MEE-tah ehl tee-YEHM-poh deh pahn-TAH-yah ah … mee-NOO-tohs
Nap time is … o'clock.	*La hora de siesta es … .* lah OH-rah deh see-YEHS-tah ehs …
Bedtime is … o'clock.	*La hora de acostarse es … .* lah OH-rah deh ah-kohs-TAHR-seh ehs
If there's a problem, call me.	*Si hay un problema, llámame.* see ahy oon proh-BLEH-mah YAH-meh-meh

Housekeeping Services

Could you … ?	*¿Podría … ?* poh-DREE-yah
change the sheets	*cambiar las sábanas* KAHM-bee-yahr lahs SAH-bahn-nahs

continues

clean the room now (later)	*asear (limpiar) la habitación ahora (más tarde)* ah-seh-YAHR (leem-pee-YAHR) lah ah-bee-tah-see-YOHN ah-OH-rah (mahs tahr-DEH)
do the laundry	*lavar la ropa* LAH-bahr lah RROH-pah
dust	*quitar el polvo* KEE-tahr ehl POHL-boh
empty the garbage pails	*vaciar los basureros* BAH-see-yahr lohs bah-soo-REH-rohs
iron the clothes	*planchar la ropa* PLAHN-chahr lah RROH-pah
load (unload) (turn on) the dishwasher	*cargar (descargar) (encender) el lavaplatos* KAHR-gahr (dehs-KAHR-gahr) (ehn-sehn-DEHR) ehl lah-bah-PLAH-tohs
take out the garbage	*sacar la basura* SAH-kahr lah bah-SOO-rah
(not) use bleach (fabric softener)	*(no) añadir blanqueador (suavizante)* (noh) ah-nyah-DEER blahn-keh-yah-DOHR (swah-bee-SAHN-teh)
vacuum	*pasar la aspiradora* PAH-sahr lah ahs-pee-rah-DOH-rah
wash the dishes	*lavar los platos* LAH-bahr lohs PLAH-tohs
water the plants	*regar las plantas* RREH-gahr lahs PLAHN-tahs

Concierge Services

Can I get a room upgrade?	*¿Es posible obtener una mejora de habitación?* EHS poh-SEE-bleh ohb-teh-NEHR OO-nah meh-HOH-rah deh ah-bee-tah-see-YOHN
Can you call a cab (a rideshare)?	*¿Puede llamarme un taxi (un viaje compartido)?* PWEH-deh yah-MAHR-meh oon TAHK-see (oon bee-YAH-heh kohm-pahr-TEE-doh)
What can my children do for fun?	*¿Qué diversiones hay para niños?* keh dee-behr-see-YOH-nehs ahy PAH-rah NEE-nyohs
Can you help me get a babysitter?	*¿Puede ayudarme a conseguir una niñera confiable?* PWEH-deh ah-yoo-DAHR-meh ah kohn-seh-GEER OO-nah nee-NYEH-rah kohn-fee-YAH-bleh
Can you help me celebrate …?	*¿Puede ayudarme a celebrar?* PWEH-deh ah-yoo-DAHR-meh ah seh-leh-BRAHR
a birthday	*un aniversario* oon ah-nee-behr-SAH-ree-yoh *un cumpleaños* oon koom-pleh-YAH-nyohs
an engagement	*un compromiso* oon kohm-proh-MEE-soh
a special wedding anniversary	*un aniversario de boda especial* oon ah-nee-behr-SAH-ree-yoh deh BOH-dah ehs-peh-see-YAHL
a special occasion	*una ocasión especial* OO-nah oh-kah-see-YOHN ehs-peh-see-YAHL
a wedding	*una boda* OO-nah BOH-dah

continues

Can you recommend a good ... ?	*¿Puede recomendarme un buen ... ?* PWEH-deh rreh-koh-mehn-DAHR-meh oon bwehn
nightclub	*club* kloob
restaurant (child-friendly)	*restaurante (apto para menores)* rrehs-tow-RAHN-teh (AHP-toh PAH-rah meh-NOH-rehs
tapas bar	*bar de tapas* bahr deh TAH-pahs
Can you make a reservation for me (us)?	*¿Puede hacerme (nos) una reservación?* PWEH-deh ah-SEHR-meh (nohs) OO-nah rreh-sehr-bah-see-YOHN
Can you get me tickets for ... ?	*¿Puede conseguirme entradas para ... ?* PWEH-deh kohn-seh-GEER-meh ehn-TRAH-dahs PAH-rah
this concert	*este concierto* EHS-teh kohn-see-YEHR-toh
this exhibition	*esta exposición* EHS-tah ehs-poh-see-see-YOHN
this play	*esta obra* EHS-tah OH-brah
this show	*este espectáculo* EHS-teh ehs-pehk-TAH-koo-loh
this sporting event	*este evento deportivo* EHS-teh eh-BEHN-toh deh-pohr-TEE-boh
Can you recommend a reliable tour guide?	*¿Puede recomendar un buen guía turístico?* PWEH-deh rreh-koh-mehn-DAHR oon bwehn GEE-yah too-REES-tee-koh
Where can I buy ... ?	*¿Dónde puedo comprar ... ?* DOHN-deh PWEH-doh kohm-PRAHR

clothing	*ropa* RROH-pah
gifts	*regalos* rreh-GAH-lohs
souvenirs	*recuerdos* rreh-KWEHR-dohs
handicrafts	*artesanías* ahr-teh-sah-NEE-yahs
jewelry	*joyas* HOH-yahs
a phone charger	*un cargador de celular* *(móvil [Spain])* oon kahr-gah-DOHR deh seh-loo-LAHR (MOH-beel)
Could you please print out my (our) boarding pass(es)?	*¿Puede imprimir mi* *(nuestras) tarjeta(s) de* *embarque?* PWEH-deh eem-pree-MEER mee (NWEHS-trahs) tahr-HEH- tah(s) deh ehm-BAHR-keh

Problems, Complaints, and Concerns

There's a problem.	*Hay un problema.* ahy oon proh-BLEH-mah
There's no …	*No hay …* noh ahy
cold water.	*agua fría.* AH-gwah FREE-yah
electricity.	*electricidad.* eh-lehk-tree-see-DAHD
heat.	*calefacción.* kah-leh-fahk-see-YOHN
hot water.	*agua caliente.* AH-gwah kah-lee-YEHN-teh
running water.	*agua corriente.* AH-gwah koh-rree-YEHN- teh

continues

The ... doesn't work.	... *no funciona.* noh foon-see-YOH-nah
air-conditioning	*el aire acondicionado* ehl AHY-reh ah-kohn-dee-see-yoh-NAH-doh
cable	*el cable* ehl KAH-bleh
elevator	*el ascensor* ehl ah-sehn-SOHR
fan	*el ventilador* ehl behn-tee-lah-DOHR
faucet	*el grifo* ehl GREE-foh
Internet	*el Internet* ehl Internet
lamp (light)	*la lámpara* lah LAHM-pah-rah
radio	*la radio* lah RRAH-dee-yoh
refrigerator	*el refrigerador* ehl rreh-free-heh-rah-DOHR
safe	*la caja fuerte* lah KAH-hah FWEHR-teh
socket	*el enchufe* ehl ehn-CHOO-feh
switch	*el interruptor* ehl een-teh-rroop-TOHR
television	*el televisor* ehl teh-leh-bee-SOHR
Wi-Fi	*el WiFi* ehl Wi-Fi
Could you fix it as soon as possible?	*¿Podría arreglarlo lo más pronto posible?* poh-DREE-yah ah-rreh-GLAHR-loh loh mahs PROHN-toh poh-SEE-bleh
We need an exterminator.	*Necesitamos un exterminador.* neh-seh-see-TAH-mohs oon ehs-tehr-mee-nah-DOHR
There are ...	*Hay ...* ahy

bedbugs.	*chinches.* CHEEN-chehs
bees.	*abejas.* ah-BEH-hahs
insects.	*insectos.* een-SEHK-tohs
mice.	*ratones.* RRAH-toh-nehs
Can I block certain television channels?	*¿Hay bloqueo de canales?* ahy bloh-KEH-yoh deh kah-NAH-lehs

Checking Out

I'd like the bill please.	*La cuenta por favor.* lah KWEHN-tah pohr fah-BOHR
Do you accept credit cards?	*¿Acepta tarjetas de crédito?* ah-SEHP-tah tahr-HEH-tahs deh KREH-dee-toh
I think there's a mistake with the bill.	*Creo que hay un error en la cuenta.* KREH-yoh keh ahy oon eh-RROHR ehn lah KWEHN-tah
I lost the key.	*Perdí la llave.* pehr-DEE lah YAH-beh
I'll (We'll) be checking out tomorrow.	*Voy (Vamos) a marcharme (nos) mañana.* boy (BAH-mohs) ah mahr-CHAHR-meh (nohs) mah-NYAH-nah
Please send for the bellhop.	*Por favor mande al botones.* pohr fah-BOHR MAHN-deh ahl boh-TOH-nehs

Other Accommodations

I'd like to rent ...	*Me gustaría alquilar ...* meh goos-tah-REE-yah ahl-kee-LAHR
an apartment.	*un apartamento.* oon ah-pahr-tah-MEHN-toh

a cabin.	*una cabaña.* OO-nah kah-BAH-nyah
a condo.	*un piso (un departamento).* oon PEE-soh (oon deh-pahr-tah-MEHN-toh)
a house.	*una casa.* OO-nah KAH-sah
I'd like to stay in a bed and breakfast.	*Me gustaría quedarme en un alojamiento y desayuno.* meh goos-tah-REE-yah keh-DAHR-meh ehn oon ah-loh-hah-mee-YEHN-toh ee deh-sah-YOO-noh
How much does it cost per day (week) (month)?	*¿Cuánto cuesta por día (semana) (mes)?* KWAHN-toh KWEHS-tah pohr DEE-yah (seh-MAH-nah) (mehs)
Is … included?	*¿Está incluido … ?* ehs-TAH een-KLWEE-doh …
air-conditioning	*la climatización* lah klee-mah-tee-sah-see-YOHN
electricity	*la electricidad* lah eh-lehk-tree-see-DAHD
gas	*el gas* ehl gahs
heat	*la calefacción* lah kah-leh-fahk-see-YOHN
How many rooms (bedrooms) (bathrooms) are there?	*¿Cuántos cuartos (dormitorios) (baños) hay?* KWAHN-tohs KWAHR-tohs (dohr-mee-TOH-ree-yohs) (BAH-nyohs) ahy
Can we park our RV at this campsite?	*¿Podemos estacionar nuestra caravana en este campamento?* poh-DEH-mohs ehs-tah-see-yoh-NAHR NWEHS-trah kah-rah-BAH-nah ehn EHS-teh kahm-pah-MEHN-toh

How much does it cost per night?	*¿Cuánto cuesta por noche?* KWAHN-toh KWEHS-tah pohr NOH-cheh
Is (Are) there ... ?	*¿Hay ...* ahy
cooking facilities	*instalaciones para cocinar* een-stah-lah-see-YOH-nehs PAH-rah koh-see-NAHR
drinking water	*agua potable* AH-gwah poh-TAH-bleh
electricity	*electricidad* eh-lehk-tree-see-DAHD
a picnic area	*una área de picnic* OO-nah AH-reh-yah deh peek-neek
a playground	*un parque infantil* oon PAHR-keh een-fahn-TEEL
showers	*duchas* DOO-chahs
toilet facilities	*servicios* sehr-BEE-see-yohs

Food

Whether you stop by a local bodega or specialty
store to grab a bite to tide you over or you make
reservations at the fanciest of restaurants, you need
to know how to ask for the foods you want and to
refuse those that don't appeal to you. You also want
to ensure you order the proper quantity. This
chapter will help you satisfy all your cravings.

Meals

The Spanish-speaking world boasts a diversified
cuisine influenced by its varied cultures. Because
each country has its own specialties, the following
phrases are general and intended to help you
navigate a menu no matter where you travel.

Breakfast, *el desayuno* (ehl deh-sah-YOO-noh), is
much lighter than its American counterpart,
consisting of coffee with milk and bread with butter
or jam. *Churros* (CHOO-rrohs), fritters made by
frying long strips of dough in oil and then sprinkling
them with sugar, and hot chocolate (*chocolate*, choh-
koh-LAH-teh) are special favorites.

Regional snacks (such as a taco) and drinks (*batidas* [bah-TEE-dahs] and *licuados* [lee-KWAH-dohs]) might be consumed midmorning.

Lunch, *la comida* (lah koh-MEE-dah) in Spain and Mexico and *el almuerzo* (ehl ahl-MWEHR-soh) in South America and the Caribbean, is considered the main meal of the day. It includes soup, meat or fish, vegetables, salad, and dessert.

La merienda (lah meh-ree-YEHN-dah), a late afternoon snack, generally consists of coffee or tea and pastry.

Supper is referred to as *la cena* (lah SEH-nah) in Spain and as *la comida* (lah koh-MEE-dah) in Spanish America. This meal tends to be light because it's consumed late, sometimes after 9:00 p.m.

At a Restaurant

If you're looking for a place to eat, you might want to select from the following.

Un bar (oon bahr), *una tasca* (OO-nah TAHS-kah), and *una taberna* (OO-nah tah-BEHR-nah) are similar to American bars where drinks and small snacks are served. *Un bar de tapas* (oon bahr deh TAH-pahs) is a popular gathering place.

Un café (oon kah-FEH) is a casual eatery that serves alcoholic and non-alcoholic drinks and plain snacks.

Una cafetería (OO-nah kah-feh-teh-REE-yah) is an informal restaurant specializing in sandwiches, snacks, coffee, and tea.

Una fonda (OO-nah FOHN-dah), *una hostería*
(OO-nah ohs-teh-REE-yah), *una venta* (OO-nah
BEHN-tah), and *una posada* (OO-nah poh-SAH-dah)
are inns that serve regional dishes.

Un restaurante (oon rrehs-tow-RAHN-teh) is
a traditional restaurant. Restaurants might have
a special price-fixed menu called *Plato Combinado*
(PLAH-toh kohm-bee-NAH-doh), *Menú Turístico*
(meh-NOO too-REES-tee-koh), or *Menú del Día*
(meh-NOO dehl DEE-yah). The bill often
indicates that a 10 to 15% tip is included (*servicio
incluido*, sehr-BEE-see-yoh een-KLWEE-doh).
It's customary to leave some additional small
change. If you feel the service went above and
beyond, a larger tip is recommended.

Un restaurante de comida rápida (oon rrehs-tow-
RAHN-teh deh koh-MEE-dah RRAH-pee-dah) is
the standard fast-food restaurant popular in the
United States.

Making Reservations

Can you recommend a good … restaurant …?	¿*Puede recomendarme un buen restaurante?* PWEH-deh rreh-koh-mehn-DAHR-meh oon bwehn rrehs-tow-RAHN-teh
vegetarian	*vegetariano* beh-heh-tah-ree-YAH-noh
vegan	*vegano* beh-GAH-noh
serving native dishes	*típico* TEE-pee-koh

continues

I'd like to reserve a table ... please.	*Me gustaría hacer una reservación ... por favor.* meh goos-tah-REE-yah ah-SEHR OO-nah rreh-sehr-bah-see-YOHN pohr fah-BOHR
for this evening	*para esta noche* PAH-rah EHS-tah NOH-cheh
for tomorrow evening	*para mañana por la noche* PAH-rah mah-NYAH-nah pohr lah NOH-cheh
for Saturday evening	*para el sábado por la noche* PAH-rah ehl SAH-bah-doh pohr lah NOH-cheh
for two (four) people	*para dos (cuatro) personas* PAH-rah dohs (KWAH-troh) pehr-SOH-nahs
for 8:30 p.m.	*para las ocho y media* PAH-rah lahs OH-choh ee MEH-dee-yah
inside	*adentro* ah-DEHN-troh
outside	*afuera* ah-FWEH-rah
on the terrace	*en la terraza* ehn lah teh-RRAH-sah
in a (quiet) corner	*en un rincón (tranquilo)* ehn oon rreen-KOHN (trahn-KEE-loh)
near the window	*cerca de la ventana* SEHR-kah deh lah behn-TAH-nah
far from the door	*lejos de la puerta* leh-HOHS deh lah PWEHR-tah
far from kitchen	*lejos de la cocina* LEH-hohs deh lah koh-SEE-nah
Is there a dress code?	*¿Hay un código de vestimenta?* ahy oon KOH-dee-goh deh behs-tee-MEHN-tah

| Do I have to wear a jacket? | *¿Tengo que usar una chaqueta? (un saco* [Latin America]*)*
 TEHN-goh keh oo-SAHR OO-nah chah-KEH-tah (oon SAH-koh) |

At the Bar

Served in *cervezerías* (sehr-beh-seh-REE-yahs) (beer houses), beer is very popular in Spain.

Please bring me a ...	*Por favor traígame ...* poh fah-BOHR TRAHY-gah-meh
small glass.	*una caña.* OO-nah KAH-nyah
bottle.	*una botella.* OO-nah boh-TEH-yah
cup.	*una copa.* OO-nah KOH-pah
large jar.	*una jarra.* OO-nah HAH-rah
pint.	*una pinta.* OO-nah PEEN-tah

Mixed drinks, *cubatas* (koo-BAH-tahs), are generally simple. For example, rum and coke, scotch and soda, or gin and tonic. You should order the specific brand of alcohol you prefer.

Wine is generally ordered with lunch or dinner.

Latin American and Mexican drinks include:

- *Cuba libre*: rum, Coca-Cola, and lime juice
- *Margarita*: tequila, lime juice, and salt
- *Piña colada*: pineapple juice, cream of coconut, and rum

- *Ponche* (POHN-cheh): fruit juice with rum or tequila

- *Pulque* (POOL-keh): fermented sap of the agave (maguey) plant

- *Tequila sunrise*: tequila, orange juice, and grenadine

Tapas

Tapas (TAH-pahs) are hot or cold small Spanish or Latin American appetizers or snacks. A combination of tapas can make a complete meal.

Where's the nearest tapas bar?	*¿Dónde está el bar de tapas más cercano?* DOHN-deh ehs-TAH ehl bahr deh TAH-pahs mahs sehr-KAH-noh
I'd like to have the ...	*Me gustaría tomar ...* meh goos-tah-REE-yah toh-MAHR
artichokes.	*las alcachofas.* lahs ahl-kah-CHOH-fahs
avocado spread.	*el guacamole.* ehl gwah-kah-MOH-leh
cheese.	*el queso.* ehl KEH-soh
clams.	*las almejas.* lahs ahl-MEH-hahs
crayfish.	*los cangrejos.* lohs kahn-GREH-hohs
eggs.	*los huevos.* lohs HWEH-bohs
meatballs.	*las albóndigas.* lahs ahl-BOHN-dee-gahs
melon.	*el melón.* ehl meh-LOHN

mushrooms.	*los champiñones.* lohs chahm-pee-NYOH-nehs
mussels.	*los mejillones.* lohs meh-hee-YOH-nehs
octopus.	*el pulpo.* ehl POOL-poh
olives.	*las aceitunas.* lahs ah-seh-yee-TOO-nahs
oysters.	*las ostras.* lahs OHS-trahs
prawns.	*las gambas.* lahs GAHM-bahs
sardines.	*las sardinas.* lahs sahr-DEE-nahs
shrimp.	*los camarones.* lohs kah-mah-ROH-nehs
smoked eels.	*las anguilas ahumadas.* lahs ahn-GEE-lahs ah-oo-MAH-dahs
snails.	*los caracoles.* lohs kah-rah-KOH-lehs
spicy sausage.	*el chorizo.* choh-REE-soh
squid.	*los calamares.* lohs kah-lah-MAH-rehs
tortilla chips.	*las tostadas.* lahs tohs-TAH-dahs

In the Restaurant

| We (I) have a reservation. | *Tenemos (Tengo) una reservación.*
teh-NEH-mohs (TEHN-goh) OO-nah rreh-sehr-bah-see-YOHN |
| (How long) Will we (I) have to wait? | *¿(Cuánto tiempo) Tendremos (tendré) que esperar?*
(KWAHN-toh tee-YEHM-poh) tehn-DREH-mohs (tehn-DREH) keh ehs-peh-RAHR |

continues

Is there a cover charge?	*¿Hay un cubierto?* ahy oon koo-bee-YEHR-toh
Where are the bathrooms?	*¿Dónde están los baños/los servicios?* [Spain] DOHN-deh ehs-TAHN lohs BAH-nyohs/lohs sehr-BEE-see-yohs
This has a chip.	*Esto tiene una desportilladura.* EHS-toh tee-YEH-neh OO-nah dehs-pohr-tee-yah-DOO-rah
This is dirty.	*Esto está sucio.* EHS-toh ehs-TAH SOO-see-yoh
I need a ...	*Necesito ...* neh-seh-SEE-toh
bowl.	*un tazón.* oon tah-SOHN
cup.	*una taza.* OO-nah TAH-sah
fork.	*un tenedor.* oon teh-neh-DOHR
glass.	*un vaso.* oon BAH-soh
knife.	*un cuchillo.* oon koo-CHEE-yoh
menu.	*un menú (una carta).* oon meh-NOO (OO-nah KAHR-tah)
napkin.	*una servilleta.* OO-nah sehr-bee-YEH-tah
place setting.	*un cubierto.* oon koo-bee-YEHR-toh
plate.	*un plato.* oon PLAH-toh
saucer.	*un platillo.* oon plah-TEE-yoh
soup dish.	*un sopero.* oon soh-PEH-roh
soup spoon.	*una cuchara.* OO-nah koo-CHAH-rah

tablecloth.	*un mantel.* oon mahn-TEHL
teaspoon.	*una cucharita.* OO-nah koo-chah-REE-tah
wine glass.	*una copa.* OO-nah KOH-pah
Please bring us (me) the menu.	*¿Nos (Me) puede traer el menú (la carta) por favor?* nohs (meh) PWEH-deh trah-YEHR ehl meh-NOO (lah KAHR-tah) pohr fah-BOHR
Please bring us (me) some bread.	*¿Nos (Me) puede traer pan por favor?* nohs (meh) PWEH-deh trah-YEHR pahn pohr fah-BOHR
Do you have a menu in English?	*¿Tiene un menú (una carta) en inglés?* tee-YEH-neh oon meh-NOO (OO-nah KAHR-tah) ehn een-GLEHS
Do you have a children's menu?	*¿Tiene un menú (una carta) para niños?* tee-YEH-neh oon meh-NOO (OO-nah KAHR-tah) PAH-rah NEE-nyohs
We'd (I'd) like the fixed-price menu.	*Nos (Me) gustaría el menú (la carta) de precio fijo.* nohs (meh) goos-tah-REE-yah ehl meh-NOO (lah KAHR-tah) deh PREH-see-yoh FEE-hoh
What's today's special?	*¿Cuál es el plato del día?* kwahl ehs ehl PLAH-toh dehl DEE-yah
What's the house specialty?	*¿Cuál es la especialidad de la casa?* kwahl ehs lah ehs-peh-see-yah-lee-DAHD deh lah KAH-sah
What do you recommend?	*¿Qué nos recomienda?* keh nohs rreh-koh-mee-YEHN-dah
We (I) would like to order.	*Nos (Me) gustaría ordenar.* nohs (meh) goos-tah-REE-yah ohr-deh-NAHR

Understanding the Menu

The following culinary terms are for foods that are served primarily in Mexico.

Sauces (Salsas)

ají de queso ah-HEE deh KEH-soh	cheese sauce
adobo ah-DOH-boh	chili sauce made with sesame seeds, nuts, and spices
mole MOH-leh	chili sauce made with sesame seeds, cocoa, and spices
pipían pee-pee-YAHN	chili and pumpkin seed sauce spiced with coriander and served with breadcrumbs
salsa cruda SAHL-sah KROO-dah	an uncooked tomato sauce dip
salsa de tomatillo SAHL-sah deh toh-mah-TEE-yoh	Mexican green tomato sauce
salsa de perejil verde SAHL-sah deh peh-reh-HEEL BEHR-deh	parsley, green chili, and green tomato sauce

Chilies (Chiles)

ancho AHN-choh	medium hot
chipotle chee-POHT-leh	hot, smoky-flavored
jalapeño hah-lah-PEH-nyoh	hot, meaty-flavored
pasilla pah-SEE-yah	hot, rich, sweet-flavored
pequín peh-KEEN	hot

pimiento pee-mee-YEHN-toh	peppery
poblano poh-BLAH-noh	medium hot, rich-flavored
serrano seh-RRAH-noh	hot

Tortillas

burrito boo-REE-toh	flour tortilla with a cheese and meat filling and served with salsa
chalupas chah-LOO-pahs	cheese- or ground pork–filled tortillas served with a green chili sauce
chilaquiles chee-lah-KEE-lehs	baked layers of tortillas filled alternately with beans, meat, chicken, and cheese
enchiladas ehn-chee-LAH-dahs	soft corn tortillas filled with meat, rice, and cheese and topped with spicy sauce
flautas FLOW-tahs	rolled, flute-shaped, deep-fried tortilla snacks
quesadillas keh-sah-DEE-yahs	stove-grilled tortillas filled with cheese and sometimes meats, vegetables, and spices
tacos TAH-kohs	crisp fried tortillas filled with meat, poultry, or beans and topped with shredded lettuce, cheese, and sauce
tostada tohs-TAH-dah	tortilla chips with different pepper and cheese toppings

Paellas

Paellas (pah-YEH-yahs) are saffron-flavored rice dishes whose ingredients vary depending on the region of Spain from which they originate.

Paella Valenciana contains chicken, pork, and tomatoes and might also contain rabbit.

Paella de Marisco is a seafood paella that doesn't contain meat.

Paella Mixta is a combo of *paella Valenciana* and *paella de Marisco*, prepared with meat and seafood.

Paella Vegetariana contains many vegetables and doesn't contain meat or seafood.

Paella Negra is black in appearance because it's prepared with squid ink.

Ordering a Meal

Soups

What's the soup of the day?	*¿Cuál es la sopa del día?* kwahl ehs lah SOH-pah dehl DEE-yah
I'll have …	*Tomo …* TOH-moh
puréed uncooked vegetable soup, served cold.	*gazpacho.* gahs-PAH-choh
thick, hearty vegetable soup or stew.	*potaje.* poh-TAH-heh
garlic soup.	*sopa de ajo.* SOH-pah deh AH-hoh
meatball soup.	*sopa de albóndigas.* SOH-pah deh ahl-BOHN-dee-gahs

onion soup.	*sopa de cebolla.* SOH-pah deh seh-BOH-yah
noodle soup.	*sopa de fideos.* SOH-pah deh fee-DEH-yohs
shrimp soup.	*sopa de gambas* *(camarones).* SOH-pah deh GAHM-bahs (kah-mah-ROH-nehs)
seafood soup.	*sopa de mariscos.* SOH-pah deh mah-REES-kohs
fish soup.	*sopa de pescado.* SOH-pah deh pehs-KAH-doh
soup made from puréed green vegetables.	*sopa de verduras.* SOH-pah deh behr-DOO-rahs

Salads

Bring me a green salad please.	*Tráigame por favor una* *ensalada verde.* TRAHY-gah-meh pohr fah-BOHR OO-nah ehn-sah-LAH-dah BEHR-deh
I'd like a mixed salad.	*Me gustaría una ensalada* *mixta.* meh goos-tah-REE-yah OO-nah ehn-sah-LAH-dah MEES-tah

Meats

I'd like ...	*Me gustaría ...* meh goos-tah-REE-yah
the beef.	*la carne de vaca.* lah KAHR-neh deh BAH-kah
the filet mignon.	*el filete miñón, el bife de* *lomo* [Argentina]. ehl fee-LEH-teh mee-NYOHN, ehl BEE-feh deh LOH-moh

continues

the ham.	*el jamón.* ehl hah-MOHN
a hamburger.	*una hamburguesa.* OO-nah ahm-boor-GEH-sah
the lamb.	*la carne de cordero.* lah KAHR-neh deh kohr-DEH-roh
the lamb chops.	*chuletas de cordero.* choo-LEH-tahs deh kohr-DEH-roh
the rack of lamb.	*la costilla de cordero.* lah kohs-TEE-yah deh kohr-DEH-roh
the liver.	*el hígado.* ehl EE-gah-doh
the meatballs.	*las albóndigas.* lahs ahl-BOHN-dee-gahs
the pork.	*el cerdo.* ehl SEHR-doh
a pork chop.	*una chuleta de cerdo.* OO-nah choo-LEH-tah deh SEHR-doh
the roast beef.	*la carne asada.* lah KAHR-neh ah-SAH-dah
the sausage.	*el chorizo.* ehl choh-REE-soh
a steak.	*el bistec, el filete, el bife* [Argentina]. ehl bees-TEHK, ehl fee-LEH-teh, ehl BEE-feh
the stew.	*el estofado, el guiso.* ehl ehs-toh-FAH-doh, ehl GWEE-soh
the veal.	*la ternera.* lah tehr-NEH-rah
the veal scallopini.	*el escalope de ternera.* ehl ehs-kah-LOH-peh deh tehr-NEH-rah
the veal stew.	*el estofado de ternera.* ehl ehs-toh-FAH-doh deh tehr-NEH-rah

Fowl and Game

chicken (stuffed)	*el pollo (relleno)* ehl POH-yoh (rreh-YEH-noh)
a chicken breast	*una pechuga de pollo* OO-nah peh-CHOO-gah deh POH-yoh
the dark meat	*la carne oscura* lah KAHR-neh ohs-KOO-rah
the thigh	*el muslo* ehl MOOS-loh
the leg	*la pierna* lah pee-YEHR-nah
duck	*el pato* ehl PAH-toh
rabbit	*el conejo* ehl koh-NEH-hoh
turkey (stuffed)	*el pavo (relleno)* ehl PAH-boh (rreh-YEH-noh)

Fish and Seafood

anchovy	*la anchoa* lah AHN-choh-wah
clam	*la almeja* lah ahl-MEH-hah
codfish	*el bacalao* ehl bah-kah-LAH-oh
crab	*el cangrejo* ehl kahn-GREH-hoh
flounder	*el lenguado* ehl lehn-GWAH-doh
grouper	*el mero* ehl MEH-roh
lobster	*la langosta* lah lahn-GOHS-tah
mackerel	*la caballa* lah kah-BAH-yah
monkfish	*el rape* ehl RRAH-peh

continues

mussels	*los mejillones* lohs meh-hee-YOH-nehs
octopus	*el pulpo* ehl POOL-poh
oysters	*las ostras* lahs OHS-trahs
prawns	*los langostinos (las gambas)* lohs lahn-gohs-TEE-nohs (lahs GAHM-bahs)
red snapper	*el pargo colorado* ehl PAHR-goh koh-loh-RAH-doh
scallops	*las conchas de peregrino* lahs KOHN-chahs deh peh-reh-GREE-noh
sea bass	*el róbalo* ehl RROH-bah-loh
shrimp	*los camarones, las gambas* lohs kah-mah-ROH-nehs, lahs GAHM-bahs
sole	*el lenguado* ehl lehn-GWAH-doh
squid	*los calamares* lohs kah-lah-MAH-rehs
swordfish	*el pez espada* ehl pehs ehs-PAH-dah
trout	*la trucha* lah TROO-chah
tuna	*el atún* ehl ah-TOON

Food Preparation

I prefer it ...	*Lo (La) prefiero ...* loh (lah) preh-fee-YEH-roh
baked.	*al horno.* ahl OHR-noh
boiled.	*hervido(a).* ehr-BEE-doh (dah)
breaded.	*empanado(a).* ehm-pah-NAH-doh (dah)

broiled.	*a la parrilla.* ah lah pah-RREE-yah
browned.	*al horno.* ahl OHR-noh
chopped.	*picado(a).* pee-KAH-doh (dah)
fried.	*frito(a).* FREE-toh (tah)
grilled.	*asado(a) a la parrilla.* ah-SAH-doh (dah) ah lah pah-RREE-yah
marinated.	*escabechado(a).* ehs-kah-beh-CHAH-doh (dah)
mashed.	*puré.* poo-REH
poached.	*escalfado(a).* ehs-kahl-FAH-doh (dah)
roasted.	*asado(a).* ah-SAH-doh (dah)
with sauce.	*con salsa.* kohn SAHL-sah
sautéed.	*salteado(a).* sahl-teh-YAH-doh (dah)
smoked.	*ahumado(a).* ah-oo-MAH-doh (dah)
steamed.	*al vapor.* ahl bah-POHR
stewed.	*estofado(a).* ehs-toh-FAH-doh (dah)
very rare.	*casi crudo(a).* kah-see KROO-doh (dah)
rare.	*poco(a) cocido(a) (poco [a]* *hecho [a])* POH-koh (kah) koh-SEE- doh (dah) (POH-koh [kah] EH-choh [chah])
medium rare.	*a punto.* ah POON-toh
medium.	*medio(a) cocido(a).* MEH-dee-yoh (yah) koh- SEE-doh [dah]

continues

medium well done	*medio(a) bien hecho(a)* MEH-dee-yoh bee-YEHN EH-choh
well done.	*bien asado(a) (hecho [a],* *cocido [a]).* bee-YEHN ah-SAH-doh (dah) (EH-choh [chah], koh- SEE-doh [dah])
a grilled steak	*un filete asado* oon fee-LEH-teh ah-SAH-doh
I prefer it grilled.	*Lo prefiero asado.* loh preh-fee-YEH-roh ah-SAH- doh
a grilled hamburger	*una hamburguesa asada* OO-nah ahm-boor-GEH-sah ah-SAH-dah
I prefer it grilled.	*La prefiero asada.* lah preh-fee-YEH-roh ah-SAH- dah
grilled prawns	*los langostinos asados* lohs lahn-gohs-TEE-nohs ah- SAH-dos
I prefer them grilled.	*Los prefiero asados.* lohs preh-fee-YEH-roh ah- SAH-dohs
grilled lobsters	*las langostas asadas* lahs lahn-GOHS-tahs ah-SAH- dahs
I prefer them grilled.	*Las prefiero asadas.* lahs preh-fee-YEH-roh ah- SAH-dahs

Vegetables

I'll have ...	*Tomo ...* TOH-moh
I don't want ...	*No quiero ...* noh kee-YEH-roh

asparagus.	*espárragos.* ehs-PAH-rrah-gohs
beans (green).	*judías.* [Spain] hoo-DEE-yahs
	ejotes. [Mexico] eh-HOH-tehs
	porotos verdes. (Chile) poh-ROH-tohs BEHR-dehs
	habichuelas. (elsewhere) ah-bee-CHWEH-lahs
beets.	*remolachas.* rreh-moh-LAH-chahs
broccoli.	*brócoli.* BROH-koh-lee
carrots.	*zanahorias.* sah-nah-OH-ree-yahs
cauliflower.	*coliflor.* koh-lee-FLOHR
celery.	*apio.* AH-pee-yoh
chickpeas.	*garbanzos.* gahr-BAHN-sohs
corn.	*maíz.* mah-YEES
cucumbers.	*pepinos.* peh-PEE-nohs
eggplant.	*berenjena.* beh-rehn-HEH-nah
lettuce.	*lechuga.* leh-CHOO-gah
mushrooms.	*champiñones.* chahm-pee-NYOH-nehs
onions.	*cebollas.* seh-BOH-yahs
peas.	*guisantes.* gwee-SAHN-tehs
peppers.	*pimientos.* pee-mee-YEHN-tohs

continues

potato (baked) (French fries).	*papa, patata (papas al horno) (papas fritas).* PAH-pah, pah-TAH-tah (PAH-pahs ahl OHR-noh) (PAH-pahs FREE-tahs)
rice.	*arroz.* ah-RROHS
spinach.	*espinaca.* ehs-pee-NAH-kah
squash.	*cucurbitácea.* koo-koor-bee-TAH-seh-yah
	calabaza. [Latin America] kah-lah-BAH-sah
sweet potato.	*papa dulce.* PAH-pah DOOL-seh
tomato.	*tomate.* toh-MAH-teh
zucchini.	*calabacín.* kah-lah-bah-SEEN

Condiments, Herbs, and Spices

Rely on menu descriptions or your server to help you determine whether a dish will be to your liking.

I like (I don't like) …	*(No) Me gusta …* (noh) meh GOOS-tah
basil.	*la albahaca.* lah ahl-bah-AH-kah
dill.	*el eneldo.* ehl eh-NEHL-doh
garlic.	*el ajo.* ehl AH-hoh
ginger.	*el jenjibre.* ehl hehn-HEE-breh
honey.	*la miel.* lah mee-YEHL
ketchup.	*la salsa de tomate.* lah SAHL-sah deh toh-MAH-teh

lemon.	*el limón.* ehl lee-MOHN
mayonnaise.	*la mayonesa.* lah meh-yoh-NEH-sah
mustard.	*la mostaza.* lah mohs-TAH-sah
oil.	*el aceite.* ehl ah-SEHY-teh
oregano.	*el orégano.* ehl oh-REH-gah-noh
paprika.	*el pimentón dulce.* ehl pee-mehn-TOHN DOOL-seh
parsley.	*perejil.* ehl peh-reh-HEEL
pepper.	*la pimienta.* lah pee-mee-YEHN-tah
rosemary.	*el romero.* ehl rroh-MEH-roh
saffron.	*el azafrán.* ehl ah-sah-FRAHN
salt.	*la sal.* lah sahl
sesame.	*el ajonjolí.* ehl ah-hohn-hoh-LEE
sugar.	*el azúcar.* ehl ah-SOO-kahr
tarragon.	*el estragón.* ehl ehs-trah-GOHN
thyme.	*el tomillo.* ehl toh-MEE-yoh
vinegar.	*el vinagre.* ehl bee-NAH-greh

Special Requests

I'm on a diet.	*Estoy a régimen (dieta).* ehs-TOY ah RREH-hee-mehn (dee-YEH-tah)

continues

I'm a vegetarian/vegan.	*Soy vegetariano(a)/vegano(a)* soy beh-heh-tah-ree-YAH-noh (nah)/beh-GAH-noh (nah)
I can't have …	*No puedo tomar …* noh PWEH-doh toh-MAHR
any dairy products.	*productos lácteos.* proh-DOOK-tohs LAHK- teh-yohs
any alcohol.	*alcohol.* ahl-koh-OHL
any saturated fats.	*grasas saturadas.* GRAH-sahs sah-too-RAH- dahs
any shellfish.	*mariscos.* mah-REES-kohs
I'm looking for a … dish … .	*Estoy buscando … un plato* … . ehs-TOY boos-KAHN-doh oon PLAH-toh
fat-free	*sin grasa* seen GRAH-sah
gluten-free	*sin gluten* seen GLOO-tehn
high in fiber.	*con mucha fibra.* kohn MOO-chah FEE-brah
low in cholesterol.	*con poco colesterol.* kohn POH-koh koh-lehs- teh-ROHL
low in fat.	*con poca grasa.* kohn POH-kah GRAH-sah
low in sodium.	*con poca sal.* kohn POH-kah sahl
non-dairy	*sin lácteos* seen LAHK-teh-yohs
non-spicy	*no picante* noh pee-KAHN-teh
organic	*orgánico* ohr-GAH-nee-koh
salt-free	*sin sal* seen sahl
sugar-free	*sin azúcar* seen ah-SOO-kahr

without artificial coloring.	*sin colorantes artificiales.* seen koh-loh-RAHN-tehs ahr-tee-fee-see-YAH-lehs
without butter (cheese, cream, garlic, onions).	*sin mantequilla (queso, crema, ajo, cebollas).* seen mahn-teh-KEE-yah (KEH-soh, KREH-mah, AH-hoh, seh-BOH-yahs)
without preservatives.	*sin conservantes.* seen kohn-sehr-BAHN-tehs

Problems

This dish is …	*Este plato está …* EHS-teh PLAH-toh ehs-TAH
cold.	*frío.* FREE-yoh
too rare.	*muy crudo.* MWEF KROO-doh
overcooked.	*sobrecocido.* soh-breh-koh-SEE-doh
burned.	*quemado.* keh-MAH-doh
too salty.	*muy salado.* mwee sah-LAH-doh
too sweet.	*muy dulce.* mwee DOOL-seh
too spicy.	*demasiado picante.* deh-mah-see-YAH-doh pee-KAHN-teh
bitter.	*amargo(a).* ah-MAHR-goh
sour.	*cortado.* kohr-TAH-doh

Beverages

| I'm thisty. | *Tengo sed.*
TEHN-goh sehd |

continues

I'd like …	*Me gustaría …* meh goos-tah-REE-yah
a beer (light, dark).	*una cerveza (clara, oscura).* OO-nah sehr-BEH-sah (KLAH-rah, ohs-KOO-rah)
coffee (decaffinated) (iced) … .	*café (descafeinado) (helado) … .* kah-FEH (dehs-kah-feh-yee-NAH-doh) (eh-LAH-doh)
with cream (milk, sugar).	*con cream (leche, azúcar).* kohn KREH-mah (LEH-cheh, ah-SOO-kahr)
an espresso.	*un espreso.* oon ehs-PREH-soh
a lemonade.	*una limonada.* OO-nah lee-moh-NAH-dah
milk.	*leche.* LEH-cheh
mineral water.	*agua mineral.* AH-gwah mee-neh-RAHL
carbonated.	*con gas.* kohn gahs
non-carbonated.	*sin gas.* seen gahs
soda (diet).	*un refresco (dietético).* oon rreh-FREHS-koh (dee-yeh-TEH-tee-koh)
tea (iced) … .	*un té (decaffeinated) (helado) … .* oon teh (dehs-kah-feh-yee-NAH-doh) (eh-LAH-doh)
with lemon (milk, sugar).	*con limón (leche, azúcar).* kohn lee-MOHN (leh-cheh, ah-SOO-kahr)
water.	*agua.* AH-gwah
(a glass of) wine.	*(una copa de) vino.* (OO-nah KOH-pah deh) BEE-noh

red wine.	*vino tinto.* BEE-noh TEEN-toh
rosé wine.	*vino rosado.* BEE-noh rroh-SAH-doh
white wine.	*vino blanco.* BEE-noh BLAHN-koh
dry wine.	*vino seco.* BEE-noh SEH-koh
sweet wine.	*vino dulce.* BEE-noh DOOL-seh
sparkling wine.	*vino espumoso.* BEE-noh ehs-poo-MOH-soh
(a glass of) (a bottle of) champagne	*(una copa de) (una botella de) champán* (OO-nah KOH-pah deh) (OO-nah boh-TEH-yah deh) chahm-PAHN
Is the water filtered?	*¿Está filtrada el agua?* ehs-TAH feel-TRAH-dah ehl AH-gwah

Desserts

I'd like to order ...	*Me gustaría ordenar ...* meh goos-tah-REE-yah ohr-deh-NAHR ...
cake.	*pastel.* pahs-TEHL
caramel custard.	*flan.* flahn
cookies.	*galletas.* gah-YEH-tahs
ice cream.	*helado.* eh-LAH-doh
a bowl of	*un bol de ... .* oon bohl deh
a ... cone.	*un cono (un cucurucho* [Argentina]*) de ...* oon KOH-noh (oon koo-koo-ROO-choh) deh

continues

vanilla	*vainilla.* vahy-NEE-yah
chocolate	*chocolate.* choh-koh-LAH-teh
strawberry	*fresa.* FREH-sah
	frutilla. [South America] froo-TEE-yah
pistachio	*pistacho.* pees-TAH-choh
pie.	*tarta.* TAHR-tah
rice pudding.	*arroz con leche.* ah-RROHS kohn LEH-cheh
sorbet.	*sorbete.* sohr-BEH-teh
a (…) tart.	*una tarta de … .* OO-nah TAHR-tah deh

Fruits

apple	*manzana* (f.) mahn-SAH-nah
apricot	*albaricoque* (m.) ahl-bah-ree-KOH-keh
banana (green)	*banana* (f.) bah-NAH-nah
	plátano (m.) PLAH-tah-noh
blackberry	*mora* (f.) MOH-rah
blueberry	*mirtilo* (m.) meer-TEE-loh
cherry	*cereza* (f.) seh-REH-sah
coconut	*coco* (m.) KOH-koh
grape	*uva* (f.) OO-bah

grapefruit	*pomelo* (m.) poh-MEH-loh
lemon	*limón* (m.) lee-MOHN
lime	*lima* (f.) LEE-mah
melon	*melón* (m.) meh-LOHN
orange	*naranja* (f.) nah-RAHN-hah
peach	*melocotón* (m.) meh-loh-koh-TOHN
pear	*pera* (f.) PEH-rah
pineapple	*piña* (f.) PEE-nyah
plum	*ciruela* (f.) see-RWEH-lah
prune	*ciruela pasa* (f.) see-RWEH-lah PAH-sah
raisin	*uva seca* (f.) OO-bah SEH-kah
raspberry	*frambuesa* (f.) frahm-BWEH-sah
strawberry	*fresa* (f.) FREH-sah
watermelon	*sandía* (f.) sahn-DEE-yah

Paying the Tab

The bill please.	*La cuenta por favor.* lah KWEHN-tah pohr fah-BOHR
Separate checks please.	*Cuentas separadas por favor.* KWEHN-tahs seh-pah-RAH-dahs pohr fah-BOHR

continues

Is the tip (service) included?	*¿Está incuida (incluido) la propina (el servicio)* ehs-TAH een-KLWEE-dah (een-KLWEE-doh) lah proh-PEE-nah (ehl sehr-BEE-see-yoh)
I think the bill is wrong.	*Me parece que la cuenta está equivocada.* meh pah-REH-seh keh lah KWEHN-tah ehs-TAH eh-kee-boh-KAH-dah
I (We) didn't order this.	*No he (hemos) pedido esto.* noh heh (EH-mohs) peh-DEE-doh EHS-toh
Thank you. Everything was delicious.	*Muchas gracias. Todo estaba delicioso.* MOO-chahs GRAH-see-yahs TOH-doh ehs-TAH-bah deh-lee-see-YOH-soh

Specialty Shops

bakery	*la panadería* lah pah-nah-deh-REE-yah
butcher shop	*la carnicería* lah kahr-nee-seh-REE-yah
candy store	*la dulcería* lah dool-seh-REE-yah
dairy store	*la lechería* lah leh-cheh-REE-yah
fish store	*la pescadería* lah pehs-kah-deh-REE-yah
fruit store	*la frutería* lah froo-teh-REE-yah
grocery (vegetable) store	*la tienda de comestibles* lah tee-YEHN-dah deh koh-mehs-TEE-blehs
liquor store	*la tienda de licores* lah tee-YEHN-dah deh lee-KOH-rehs
market	*el mercado* ehl mehr-KAH-doh
pastry shop	*la pastelería* lah pahs-teh-leh-REE-yah

| supermarket (very big) | *el supermercado (el hipermercado)*
ehl soo-pehr-mehr-KAH-doh
(ehl ee-pehr-mehr-KAH-doh) |

Quantities

In Spanish-speaking countries, the metric system is used when measuring quantities of food. Liquids are measured in liters and solids are measured in grams and kilograms. Use the following when shopping.

I need ...	*Necesito ...* neh-seh-SEE-toh
a bag of nuts.	*una bolsa (un paquete) de (nueces).* OO-nah BOHL-sah (oon pah-KEH-teh) deh (NWEH-sehs)
a bar of (chocolate).	*una tableta de (chocolate).* OO-nah tah-BLEH-tah deh (choh-koh-LAH-teh)
a bar of (soap).	*una pastilla de (jabón).* OO-nah pahs-TEE-yah deh (hah-BOHN)
a bottle of (water).	*una botella de (agua).* OO-nah boh-TEH-yah deh (AH-gwah)
a box of (cereal).	*una caja de (cereal).* OO-nah KAH-hah deh (seh-reh-YAHL)
a can of soup.	*una lata de (sopa).* OO-nah LAH-tah deh (SOH-pah)
a dozen (eggs).	*una docena de (huevos).* OO-nah doh-SEH-nah deh (HWEH-bohs)
a jar of (tomato sauce).	*un frasco de (salsa de tomate).* oon FRAHS-koh deh (SAHL-sah deh toh-MAH-teh)

continues

a liter of (milk).	*un litro de (leche).* oon LEE-troh deh (LEH-cheh)
a package of (cheese).	*un paquete de (queso).* oon pah-KEH-teh deh (KEH-soh)
a piece of (apple pie).	*un pedazo (trozo) de (tarta de manzana).* oon peh-DAH-soh (TROH-soh) deh (TAHR-tah deh mahn-SAH-nah)
a quarter pound of (butter) [about 100 grams].	*cien gramos de (mantequilla).* syehn GRAH-mohs deh (mahn-teh-KEE-yah)
a half pound of (oranges) [about 90 kilograms].	*doscientos gramos de (naranjas).* dohs-see-YEHN-tohs GRAH-mohs deh (nah-RAHN-hahs)
a pound of (grapes) [about ½ kilo].	*un medio kilo de (uvas).* oon MEH-dee-yoh KEE-loh deh (OO-bahs)
2 pounds of (turkey) [about 1 kilo].	*un kilo de pavo.* oon KEE-loh deh PAH-boh
5 pounds of (potatoes) [about 2.5 kilos].	*dos kilos y media de (papas)* dohs KEE-lohs ee MEH-dee-yoh deh PAH-pahs
a slice of (ham).	*una rebanada de (jamón).* OO-nah rreh-bah-NAH-dah deh (hah-MOHN)
a little (salt).	*un poco de (sal).* oon POH-koh deh (sahl)
a lot (of) (pepper).	*mucha (pimienta).* MOO-chah (pee-mee-YEHN-tah)
enough (sugar).	*bastante/suficiente (azúcar).* bahs-TAHN-teh/ soo-fee-see-YEHN-teh (ah-SOO-kahr)
too much (garlic).	*demasiado (ajo).* deh-mah-see-YAH-doh (AH-hoh)

Shopping

Purchases you make while traveling in a foreign
country will remind you and your loved ones of
your trip for years to come. You'll undoubtedly
want to select the perfect memento or gift—
whether it's clothing or handicrafts. No matter
what your preference, this chapter will help you
purchase those memorable items.

Stores

The following lists points you in the direction of stores (*las tiendas*, lahs tee-YEHN-dahs) that might interest you:

I am looking for a ...	*Estoy buscando ...* ehs-TOY boos-KAHN-doh
bookstore.	*una librería.* OO-nah lee-breh-REE-yah
clothing store ...	*una tienda de ropa ...* OO-nah tee-YEHN-dah deh RROh-pah
for women.	*para mujeres.* PAH-rah moo-HEH-rehs
for men.	*para hombres.* PAH-rah OHM-brehs
for children.	*para niños.* PAH-rah NEE-nyohs
department store.	*un almacén.* oon ahl-mah-SEHN
handicrafts store.	*una tienda de artesanías.* OO-nah tee-YEHN-dah deh ahr-teh-sah-NEE-yahs
jewelry store.	*una joyería.* OO-nah hoh-yeh-REE-yah
liquor store.	*una licorería.* OO-nah lee-koh-reh-REE-yah
mall.	*un centro comercial.* oon SEHN-troh koh-mehr-see-YAHL
market.	*un mercado.* oon mehr-KAH-doh
newsstand.	*un quiosco de periódicos.* oon kee-YOHS-koh deh peh-ree-YOH-dee-kohs
shoe store.	*una zapatería.* OO-nah sah-pah-teh-REE-yah

souvenir shop.	*una tienda de recuerdos.* OO-nah tee-YEHN-dah deh rreh-KWEHR-dohs
tobacco store.	*una tabaquería.* OO-nah tah-bah-keh-REE yah
toy store.	*una juguetería.* OO-nah hoo-geh-teh-REE-yah
Where is it?	*¿Dónde esta?* DOHN-deh ehs-TAH

General Questions

Where can I find … ?	*¿Dónde se puedo encontrar … ?* DOHN-deh seh PWEH-doh ehn-kohn-TRAHR
Could you please help me?	*¿Podría ayudarme por favor?* poh-DREE-yah ah-yoo-DAHR-meh pohr fah-BOHR
Do you sell … ?	*¿Se venden … ?* seh BEHN-dehn
Could you please show me … ?	*¿Podría mostrarme … por favor?* poh-DREE-yah mohs-TRAHR-meh … pohr fah-BOHR
Where is (are) … ?	*¿Dónde está(n) … ?* DOHN-deh ehs-TAH(N)
How much does it (do they) cost?	*¿Cuánto cuesta(n)?* KWAHN-toh KWEHS-tah(n)
What's the price?	*¿Cuál es el precio?* kwahl ehs ehl PREH-see-yoh
Are there any sales?	*¿Hay ventas (gangas)?* ahy BEHN-tahs (GAHN-gahs)
Is there a discount? How much is it?	*¿Hay un descuento? ¿Cuánto es?* ahy oon dehs-KWEHN-toh KWAHN-toh ehs
Where do I pay?	*¿Dónde se paga?* DOHN-deh seh PAH-gah

continues

Could you put it in a bag (box)?	*¿Podría ponerlo (la) en una bolsa (caja)?* poh-DREE-yah poh-NEHR-loh (lah) ehn OO-nah BOHL-sah (KAH-hah)
Do you accept credit (debit) cards?	*Aceptan tarjetas de crédito (débito)?* ah-SEHP-tahn tahr-HEH-tahs deh KREH-dee-toh (DEH-bee-toh)
Which ones do you accept?	*¿Cuáles aceptan?* KWAH-lehs ah-SEHP-tahn
My card has (doesn't have) a chip.	*Mi tarjeta (no) tiene un chip.* mee tahr-HEH-tah (noh) tee-YEH-neh oon cheep
Where should I insert it?	*¿Dónde debo insertarla?* DOHN-deh DEH-boh een-sehr-TAHR-lah
Where do I sign?	*¿Dónde tengo que firmar?* DOHN-deh TEHN-goh keh feer-MAHR
Can I return my purchase?	*¿Puedo devolver mi compra?* PWEH-doh deh-bohl-BEHR mee KOHM-prah
Would you please give me a receipt?	*Déme un recibo por favor.* DEH-meh oon rreh-SEE-boh pohr fah-BOHR
Could you please gift wrap this?	*¿Podría envolver esto para regalo?* poh-DREE-yah ehn-bohl-BEHR EHS-toh PAH-rah rreh-GAH-loh
Could you please send this to the United States?	*Podría enviar esto a los Estados Unidos?* poh-DREE-yah ehn-bee-YAHR EHS-toh ah lohs ehs-TAH-dohs oo-NEE-dohs

General Statements

I'm just looking.	*Estoy echando un vistazo.* ehs-TOY eh-CHAHN-doh oon bees-TAH-soh

I'm looking for ...	*Estoy buscando ...* ehs-TOY boos-KAHN-doh
I (don't) want to spend a lot.	*(No) quiero gastar mucho.* (noh) kee-YEH-roh gahs-TAHR MOO-choh
I can't find what I'm looking for.	*No puedo encontrar lo que busco.* no PWEH-doh ehn-kohn-TRAHR loh keh BOOS-koh
Show me where it is please.	*Por favor muéstreme donde está.* pohr fah-BOHR MWEHS-treh-meh DOHN-deh ehs-TAH
I'd like to return this.	*Me gustaría devolver esto.* meh goos-tah-REE-yah deh-bohl-BEHR EHS-toh
It doesn't work.	*No funciona.* no foon-see-YOH-nah
It doesn't fit me.	*No me queda bien.* no meh KEH-dah bee-YEHN
I'd like to exchange this.	*Quiero reemplazar esto.* kee-YEH-roh rreh-ehm-plah-SAHR EHS-toh
I'd like a refund please.	*Me gustaría un reembolso por favor.* meh goos-tah-REE-yah oon rreh-ehm-BOHL-soh pohr fah-BOHR
I don't want store credit.	*No quiero crédito de la tienda.* no kee-YEH-roh KREH-dee-toh deh lah tee-YEHN-dah

Bookstore and Newsstand

Do you sell ... (in English)?	*Se venden ... (en inglés)?* seh BEHN-dehn ... (ehn een-GLEHS)
books (for children).	*libros (para niños).* LEE-brohs (PAH-rah NEE-nyohs)
guides.	*guías.* GEE-yahs

continues

magazines.	*revistas.* rreh-BEES-tahs
maps.	*mapas.* MAH-pahs
newspapers.	*periódicos.* peh-ree-YOH-dee-kohs
I'd like to buy a bilingual Spanish–English pocket dictionary.	*Me gustaría comprar un diccionario de bolsillo bilingüe español–inglés.* meh goos-tah-REE-yah kohm-PRAHR oon deek-see-yoh-NAH-ree-yoh deh bohl-SEE-yoh bee-LEEN-gweh ehs-pah-NYOHL-een-GLEHS

Clothing Store

Clothing Items

I'm looking for ...	*Estoy buscando ...* ehs-TOY boos-KAHN-doh
a bathing suit.	*un traje de baño.* oon TRAH-heh deh BAH-nyoh
a belt.	*un cinturón.* oon seen-too-ROHN
a blazer (sports coat).	*un blazer.* oon BLAH-sehr
a blouse.	*una blusa.* OO-nah BLOO-sah
boots.	*botas.* BOH-tahs
a brassiere.	*un sostén.* oon sohs-TEHN
a cap.	*un gorro.* oon GOH-rroh
capris.	*pantalones pescadores.* pahn-tah-LOH-nehs pehs-kah-DOH-rehs

a dress.	*un vestido.* oon behs-TEE-doh
gloves.	*guantes.* GWAHN-tehs
a hat.	*un sombrero.* oon sohm-BREH-roh
a hoodie.	*una sudadera con capucha.* OO-nah soo-dah-DEH-rah kohn kah-POO-chah *un buzo.* oon BOO-soh
a jacket.	*una chaqueta.* OO-nah chah-KEH-tah
jeans.	*jeans (vaqueros).* jeens (bah-KEH-rohs)
an overcoat.	*un abrigo.* oon ah-BREE-goh
pajamas.	*pijamas.* pee-YAH-mahs
panties.	*bragas.* BRAH-gahs
pants.	*pantalones.* pahn-tah-LOH-nehs
pantyhose.	*pantimedias.* pahn-tee-MEH-dee-yahs
a pocketbook.	*una bolsa.* OO-nah BOHL-sah
a raincoat.	*un impermeable.* oon eem-pehr-meh-YAH-bleh
a robe.	*una bata.* OO-nah BAH-tah
sandals.	*sandalias.* sahn-DAH-lee-yahs
a scarf.	*una bufanda.* OO-nah boo-FAHN-dah
a shirt.	*una camisa.* OO-nah kah-MEE-sah

continues

shoes.	*zapatos.* sah-PAH-tohs
shorts.	*pantalones cortos.* pahn-tah-LOH-nehs KOHR-tohs
a skirt.	*una falda.* OO-nah FAHL-dah
slippers.	*pantuflas.* pahn-TOO-flahs
sneakers.	*zapatillas.* sah-pah-TEE-yahs
socks.	*calcetines.* kahl-seh-TEE-nehs
stockings.	*medias.* MEH-dee-yahs
a suit (man's).	*un traje.* oon TRAH-heh
a suit (woman's).	*un traje sastre.* oon TRAH-heh SAHS-treh
sweatpants.	*un pantalón de chándal.* oon pahn-tah-LOHN deh CHAHN-dahl
a sweatshirt.	*una sudadera.* OO-nah soo-dah-DEH-rah
a sweater.	*un suéter.* oon SWEH-tehr
a T-shirt.	*una camiseta.* OO-nah kah-mee-SEH-tah *una playera.* [Mexico] (OO-nah plah-YEH-rah) *una remera.* [South America] OO-nah rreh-MEH-rah
a tie.	*una corbata.* OO-nah kohr-BAH-tah
an umbrella.	*un paraguas.* oon pah-RAH-gwahs
an undershirt.	*una camiseta.* OO-nah kah-mee-SEH-tah

undershorts.	*calzoncillos.* kahl-sohn-SEE-yohs
underwear.	*ropa interior.* RROH-pah een-teh-ree-YOHR
I need this …	*Necesito esto …* nah-seh-SEE-toh EHS-toh
with long sleeves.	*con mangas largas.* kohn MAHN-gahs LAHR-gahs
with short sleeves.	*con mangas cortas.* kohn MAHN-gahs KOHR-tahs
sleeveless.	*sin mangas.* seen MAHN-gahs
I wear size small (medium) (large).	*Llevo talla pequeña (mediana) (grande).* YEH-boh TAH-yah peh-KEH-nyah (meh-dee-YAH-nah) (GRAHN-dch)

Colors

Do you have this in … ?	*¿Tiene esto en … ?* tee-YEH-neh EHS-toh ehn
beige	*beige* BEH-heh
black	*negro* NEH-groh
blue	*azul* ah-SOOL
brown	*marrón, pardo* mah-RROHN, PAHR-doh
gray	*gris* grees
green	*verde* BEHR-deh
navy blue	*azul marino* ah-SOOL mah-REE-noh
orange	*anaranjado* ah-nah-rahn-HAH-doh

continues

pink	*rosado* rroh-SAH-doh
purple	*morado* moh-RAH-doh
red	*rojo* RROH-hoh
white	*blanco* BLAHN-koh
yellow	*amarillo* ah-mah-REE-yoh
Do you have other colors (styles)?	*¿Tiene otros colores (estilos)?* tee-YEH-neh OH-trohs koh-LOH-rehs (ehs-TEE-lohs)
I prefer ...	*Prefiero ...* preh-fee-YEH-roh

Materials

Use *de* to ask for an article of clothing made from a specific material. For example:

I'd like to buy a cashmere sweater.

Me gustaría comprar un suéter de cachemira.
meh goos-tah-REE-yah kohm-PRAHR oon SWEH-tehr deh kah-sheh-MEE-rah

cashmere	*cachemira* kah-sheh-MEE-rah
chiffon	*gasa* GAH-sah
cotton	*algodón* ahl-goh-DOHN
denim	*jean* jeen
flannel	*franela* frah-NEH-lah
lace	*encaje* ehn-KAH-heh

leather	*cuero* KWEH-roh
linen	*lino* LEE-noh
nylon	*nailon* nahy-LOHN
permanent press	*resistente a arrugas* rreh-sees-TEHN-teh ah ah-RROO-gahs
satin	*raso (satén)* RRAH-soh (sah-TEHN)
silk	*seda* SEH-dah
suede	*gamuza* gah-MOO-sah
wool	*lana* LAH-nah

Designs

I prefer the shirt ...	*Prefiero la camisa ...* preh-fee-YEH-roh lah kah-MEE-sah
in a solid color.	*de color liso.* deh koh-LOHR LEE-soh
with pinstripes.	*de rayas diplomáticas (finas).* deh RAH-yahs dee-ploh-MAH-tee-kahs (FEE-nahs)
with stripes.	*de rayas.* deh RRAH-yahs
with polka dots.	*de lunares.* deh loo-NAH-rehs
in plaid.	*de cuadros.* deh KWAH-drohs
Can I try this on?	*¿Puedo probarme esto?* PWEH-doh proh-BAHR-meh EHS-toh
Where are the dressing rooms?	*¿Dónde están los probadores?* DOHN-deh ehs-TAHN lohs proh-bah-DOH-rehs

continues

Choices

Do you have something ... ?	*¿Tiene algo ... ?* tee-YEH-neh AHL-goh
else	*más* mahs
larger	*más grande* mahs GRAHN-deh
smaller	*más pequeño* mahs peh-KEH-nyoh
longer	*más largo* mahs LAHR-goh
shorter	*más corto* mahs KOHR-toh
less expensive	*más barato* mahs bah-RAH-toh
more expensive	*más caro* mahs KAH-roh
better quality	*de mejor calidad* deh meh-HOHR kah-lee-DAHD
Does it come in another color?	*¿Viene en otro color?* bee-YEH-neh ehn OH-troh koh-LOHR
Does it fit me?	*¿Me queda bien?* meh KEH-dah bee-YEHN
It fits (doesn't fit) me.	*(No) Me queda bien.* (noh) meh KEh-dah bee-YEHN
Can you alter it?	*¿Puede arreglarlo?* PWEH-deh ah-rreh-GLAHR-loh
When will this be ready?	*¿Cuándo estará listo?* KWAHN-doh ehs-TAH-rah LEES-toh
The zipper is stuck.	*La cremallera está atascada.* lah kreh-mah-YEH-rah ehs-TAH ah-tahs-KAH-dah
I like it (them).	*Me gusta(n).* meh GOOS-tah(n).
I'll take this.	*Llevo esto.* YEH-boh EHS-toh.

Shoes

Please show me that pair of shoes (boots).	*Por favor muéstreme este par de zapatos (botas).* pohr fah-BOHR, MWEHS-treh-meh EHS-teh pahr deh sah-PAH-tohs (BOH-tahs)
The ones with the high (medium) heels.	*Los (Las) de tacón alto (medio) (bajo).* lohs (lahs) deh tah-KOHN AHL-toh (MEH-dee-yoh) (BAH-hoh)
I'd like to see those sneakers.	*Me gustaría ver estas zapatillas.* meh goos-tah-REE-yah behr EHS-tahs sah-pah-TEE-yahs
I wear size ...	*Uso número ...* OO-soh NOO-meh-roh
Do you have them in another color?	*¿Los (Las) tiene en otro color?* lohs (lahs) tee-YEH-neh ehn OH-troh koh-LOHR
They're too big (small).	*Son demasiado grandes (pequeño[-a]s).* sohn deh-mah-see-YAH-doh GRAHN-dehs (peh-KEH-nyohs [nyah(s)])
They're too wide (narrow).	*Son demasiado ancho[-a]s (estrecho[-a]s).* sohn deh-mah-see-YAH-doh AHN-chohs [chahs] (ehs-TREH-chohs [chah(s)])
They fit me well.	*Me quedan bien.* meh KEH-dahn bee-YEHN
I'll take them.	*Me los (las) llevo.* meh lohs (lahs) YEH-boh

Jewelry

I'm looking for ...	*Busco ...* BOOS-koh
a bracelet.	*un brazalete (una pulsera).* oon brah-sah-LEH-teh (OO-nah pool-SEH-rah)

continues

a brooch.	*un broche.* oon BROH-cheh
a chain.	*una cadena.* OO-nah kah-DEH-nah
a charm.	*un dije.* oon DEE-heh
earrings.	*aretes (pendientes [Spain]).* ah-REH-tehs (pehn-dee-YEHN-tehs)
a necklace.	*un collar.* oon koh-YAHR
a ring.	*un anillo (una sortija).* oon ah-NEE-yoh (OO-nah sohr-TEE-hah)
rosary beads.	*un rosario.* oon rroh-SAH-ree-yoh
a watch.	*un reloj.* oon rreh-LOH
Is this (solid) gold?	*¿Es de oro (macizo)?* ehs deh OH-roh (mah-SEE-soh)
Is this gold-plated?	*¿Está chapado(a) en oro?* ehs-TAH chah-PAH-doh (dah) ehn OH-roh
Is this silver or silver-plated?	*¿Es de plata o está plateado(a)?* ehs deh PLAH-tah oh ehs-TAH plah-teh-YAH-doh (dah)
What's that stone?	*¿Qué es esa piedra?* keh ehs EH-sah pee-YEH-drah
Is it (Are they) ... ?	*¿Es (Son) ... ?* *ehs (sohn)*
an amethyst	*una amatista* OO-nah ah-mah-TEES-tah
an aquamarine	*un aguamarina* oon ah-gwah-mah-REE-nah
a diamond	*un diamante* oon dee-yah-MAHN-teh
an emerald	*una esmeralda* OO-nah ehs-meh-RAHL-dah

ivory	*marfil* MAHR-feel
jade	*jade* HAH-deh
an onyx	*un ónix* oon OH-neeks
pearls	*perlas* PEHR-lahs
a ruby	*un rubí* oon rroo-BEE
a sapphire	*un zafiro* oon sah-FEE-roh
a topaz	*un topacio* oon toh-PAH-see-yoh
a turquoise	*una turquesa* OO-nah toor-KEH-sah

Tobacco Store

Go to a *tabaquería* if you have smoking needs.

I'd like to buy …	*Me gustaría comprar …* meh goos-tah-REE-yah kohm-PRAHR
a pack of cigarettes.	*un paquete de cigarrillos.* oon pah-KEH-teh deh see-gah-RREE-yohs
an electronic cigarette.	*un cigarrillo electrónico.* oon see-gah-RREE-yoh eh-lehk-TROH-nee-koh
(chewing) tobacco.	*tabaco de mascar.* tah-BAH-koh deh mahs-KAHR
a box of cigars.	*una caja de cigarros.* OO-nah KAH-hah deh see-GAH-rrohs
a cigar case.	*una cigarrera.* OO-nah see-gah-RREH-rah
a lighter.	*un encendedor.* oon ehn-sehn-deh-DOHR

continues

an ashtray.	*un cenicero.* oon seh-nee-SEH-roh
a pipe.	*una pipa.* OO-nah PEE-pah
a hookah.	*una narguile.* OO-nah nahr-GEE-leh

Liquor Store

I'd like to buy a bottle of …	*Me gustaría comprar una botella de …* meh goos-tah-REE-yah kohm-PRAHR OO-nah boh-TEH-yah deh
bourbon.	*borbón.* bohr-BOHN
brandy.	*brandy (coñac).* BRAHN-dee (KOH-nyahk)
champagne.	*champán.* chahm-PAHN
gin.	*ginebra.* hee-NEH-brah
rum.	*ron.* rrohn
rye.	*whiskey de centeno.* WEES-kee deh sehn-TEH-noh
scotch.	*whisky escosés.* WEES-kee ehs-koh-SEHS
tequila.	*tequila.* teh-KEE-lah
vodka.	*vodka.* BOHD-kah
whiskey.	*whisky.* WEES-kee
wine (red) (white) (rosé).	*vino (tinto) (blanco) (rosado).* BEE-noh (TEEN-toh) (BLAHN-koh) (rroh-SAH-doh)

Is it dry (fruity)?	*Es seco (afrutado)?* ehs SEH-koh (ah-froo-TAH-doh)
Do you sell bottle openers (corkscrew)?	*¿Vende sacacorchos (abrebotellas)?* BEHN-deh sah-kah-KOHR-chohs (ah-breh-boh-TEH-yahs)
Do you sell wine bottle openers?	*¿Vende tirabuzones (destapadores)?* BEHN-deh tee-rah-boo-SOH-nehs (dehs-tah-pah-DOH-rehs)

Gifts and Souvenirs

Where can I buy typical gifts (souvenirs)?	*¿Dónde puedo comprar regalos (recuerdos) típicos?* DOHN-deh PWEH-doh kohm-PRAHR rreh-GAH-lohs (rreh-KWEHR-dohs) TEE-pee-kohs
I'd like to buy a gift for my ...	*Me gustaría comprar un regalo para mi ...* meh goos-tah-REE-yah kohm-PRAHR oon rreh-GAH-loh PAH-rah mee
What do you suggest?	*¿Qué me sugiere?* keh meh soo-hee-YEH-reh
Please show me ...	*Por favor muéstreme ...* pohr fah-BOHR MWEHS-treh-meh
dolls.	*muñecas.* moo-NYEH-kahs
earthenware.	*loza.* LOH-sah
fans.	*abanicos.* ah-bah-NEE-kohs
leather wine bottles.	*botas.* BOH-tahs
masks.	*máscaras.* MAHS-kah-rahs
musical instruments.	*instrumentos musicales.* een-stroo-MEHN-tohs moo-see-KAH-lehs

continues

perfumes.	*perfumes.* pehr-FOO-mehs
posters.	*carteles.* kahr-TEH-lehs
pottery.	*cerámica.* seh-RAH-mee-kah
scarves.	*pañuelos.* pah-nyoo-WEH-lohs
silver jewelry.	*joyería de plata.* hoh-yeh-REE-yah deh PLAH-tah
tablecloths.	*manteles.* mahn-TEH-lehs
T-shirts.	*camisetas (playeras,* *[Mexico]).* kah-mee-SEH-tahs (plah- YEH-rahs

Bargaining

How much is this?	*¿Cuánto cuesta?* KWAHN-toh KWEHS-tah
That's too expensive.	*Es muy caro.* ehs mwee KAH-roh
Could you lower the price?	*¿Podría bajar el precio?* poh-DREE-yah bah-HAHR ehl PREH-see-yoh
I'll give you ...	*Le daré ...* leh dah-REH
Will you accept ... ?	*¿Aceptaría ... ?* ah-sehp-tah-REE-yah
That's good.	*Está bien.* ehs-TAH bee-YEHN
We have a deal.	*Tenemos un trato.* teh-NEH-mohs oon TRAH-toh
It's a bargain.	*Es una ganga.* ehs OO-nah GAHN-gah

Chapter 9

Sightseeing & Entertainment

Do you plan to go it alone or do you prefer to take a tour? Are you heading to the sea to engage in water sports, up to the mountains for skiing or hiking, onto the links for a round of golf, or onto the courts for tennis? Are you a film buff or a theatergoer or do you enjoy a lively opera or an elegant ballet? Perhaps you'll spend some time with a one-armed bandit in a luxurious casino. This chapter will help you partake in all these leisure activities.

Getting Information

Where's a tourist office?	*¿Dónde hay una oficina de turismo?* DOHN-deh ahy OO-nah oh-fee-SEE-nah deh too-REES-moh
What's there to see?	*¿Qué hay para ver?* keh ahy PAH-rah behr
Where can I buy a map (a guidebook)?	*¿Dónde puedo comprar un mapa (una guía)?* DOHN-deh PWEH-doh kohm-PRAHR oon MAH-pah (OO-nah GEE-yah)
What do you recommend we (I) see?	*¿Qué recomienda que veamos (vea)?* keh rreh-koh-mee-YEHN-dah que BEH-yah-mohs (BEH-yah)
I need a guide who speaks English.	*Necesito un guía que hable inglés.* neh-seh-SEE-toh oon GEE-yah keh AH-bleh een-GLEHS
How much does he (she) charge … ?	*¿Cuánto cobra … ?* KWAHN-toh KOH-brah
by the hour.	*por hora.* pohr OH-rah
by the day.	*por día.* pohr DEE-yah
per person.	*por persona.* pohr pehr-SOH-nah
I'd like to speak to him (her).	*Me gustaría hablarle.* meh goos-tah-REE-yah ah-BLAHR-leh

Attractions

We (I) would like to see the …	*Nos (Me) gustaría ver …* nohs (meh) goos-tah-REE-yah behr
aquarium.	*el acuario.* ehl ah-KWAH-ree-yoh

business center.	*el centro comercial.* ehl SEHN-troh koh-mehr-see-YAHL
castle.	*el castillo.* ehl kahs-TEE-yoh
cathedral.	*la cathedral.* lah kah-teh-DRAHL
church.	*la iglesia.* lah ee-GLEH-see-yah
downtown.	*el centro.* ehl SEHN-troh
fountain.	*la fuente.* lah FWEHN-teh
main square.	*la plaza central.* lah PLAH-sah SEHN-trahl
market.	*el mercado.* ehl mehr-KAH-doh
museum.	*el museo.* ehl moo-SEH-yoh
old city.	*la ciudad vieja.* lah see-yoo-DAHD bee-YEH-hah
opera.	*la ópera.* lah OH-peh-rah
palace.	*el palacio.* ehl pah-LAH-see-yoh
park.	*el parque.* ehl PAHR-keh
ruins.	*las ruinas.* lahs RWEE-nahs
zoo.	*el parque zoológico.* ehl PAHR-keh soo-oh-LOH-hee-koh
Is there a guided tour?	*¿Hay una visita guiada?* ahy OO-nah bee-SEE-tah gee-YAH-dah
At what time?	*¿A qué hora?* ah keh OH-rah?
Where does it leave from?	*¿De dónde sale?* deh DOHN-deh SAH-leh

continues

| How long does it last? | *¿Cuánto tiempo dura?*
KWAHN-toh tee-YEHM-poh DOO-rah? |
| At what time does it return? | *¿A qué hora vuelve?*
ah keh OH-rah BWEHL-beh |

General Tourist Admission Information

Is it handicap accessible?	*¿Hay acceso para minusválidos?* ahy ahk-SEH-soh PAH-rah mee-noos-BAH-lee-dohs
Where can I get tickets?	*¿Dónde puedo conseguir entradas?* DOHN-deh PWEH-doh kohn-seh-GEER ehn-TRAH-dahs
What days is it open (closed)?	*¿Qué días está abierto(a) (cerrado[a])?* keh DEE-yahs ehs-TAH ah-bee-YEHR-toh (tah) (seh-RRAH-doh [dah])
At what time does it open (close)?	*¿A qué hora abre (cierra)?* ah keh OH-rah AH-breh (see-YEH-rah)
What's the admission price?	*¿Cuánto cuesta la entrada?* KWAHN-toh KWEHS-tah lah ehn-TRAH-dah
Can children enter for free?	*¿Pueden entrar gratis los niños?* PWEHN-dehn ehn-trahr GRAH-tees lohs NEE-nyohs
Until what age?	*¿Hasta qué edad?* AHS-tah keh eh-DAHD
How much do they pay?	*¿Cuánto pagan?* KWAHN-toh PAH-gahn
Is there a student (senior) discount?	*¿Hay un descuento para estudiantes (mayores)?* ahy oon dehs-KWEHN-toh PAH-rah ehs-too-dee-YAHN-tehs (mah-YOH-rehs)

What's the age for seniors?	*¿Cuál es la edad para los mayores?* kwahl ehs lah eh-DAHD PAH-rah lohs mah-YOH-rehs
Is it all right to take pictures (with a flash)?	*¿Se puede sacar fotos (con flash)?* seh PWEH-deh sah-KAHR FOH-tohs kohn flahsh
Is there a dress code?	*¿Hay un código de vestimenta?* ahy oon KOH-dee-goh deh behs-tee-MEHN-tah
Are there facilities for the handicapped (blind) (deaf)?	*¿Hay servicios para los minusválidos (ciegos) (sordos)?* ahy sehr-BEE-see-yohs PAH-rah lohs mee-noos-BAH-lee-dohs (see-YEH-gohs) (SOHR-dohs)

Entertainment

Where can I buy … ?	*¿Dónde puedo comprar … ?* DOHN-deh PWEH-doh kohm-PRAHR
an entertainment guide	*una agenda cultural* OO-nah ah-HEHN-dah kool-too-RAHL
tickets	*entradas* ehn-TRAH-dahs
Is it necessary to buy tickets in advance?	*¿Es necesario comprar entradas con antelación?* ehs neh-seh-SAH-ree-yoh kohm-PRAHR ehn-TRAH-dahs kohn ahn-teh-lah-see-YOHN
Can I buy tickets online?	*¿Puedo comprar entradas por Internet?* PWEH-doh kohm-PRAHR ehn-TRAH-dahs pohr Internet?
What website gives information?	*¿Qué sitio web da información?* keh SEE-tee-yoh wehb dah een-fohr-mah-see-YOHN

continues

We (I) would like to go …	*Nos (me) gustaría ir …* nohs (meh) goos-tah-REE-yah eer
to the amusement park.	*al parque de atracciones.* ahl PAHR-keh deh ah-trahk-see-YOH-nehs
to the ballet.	*al ballet.* ahl bah-LEH
to a bullfight.	*a una corrida de toros.* ah OO-nah koh-RREE-dah deh TOH-rohs
to the carnival.	*al carnaval.* ahl kahr-nah-BAHL
to a casino.	*a un casino.* ah oon kah-SEE-noh
to the circus.	*al circo.* ahl SEER-koh
to a concert (rock/classical music).	*a un concierto (de rock/de música clásica).* ah oon kohn-see-YEHR-toh (deh rohk/deh MOO-see-kah KLAH-see-kah)
to the fair.	*a la feria.* ah lah FEH-ree-yah
to the movies.	*al cine.* ahl SEE-neh
to the opera.	*a la ópera.* ah lah OH-peh-rah
to the theater.	*al teatro.* ahl teh-YAH-troh
Is it near (far)?	*¿Está cerca (lejos)?* ehs-TAH SEHR-kah (LEH-hohs)
How do we (I) get there?	*¿Cómo llegamos (llego) allí?* KOH-moh yeh-GAH-mohs (YEH-goh) ah-YEE
What kind of film (play) are they showing?	*¿Qué tipo de película (obra) están pasando?* keh TEE-poh deh peh-LEE-koo-lah (OH-brah) ehs-TAHN pah-SAHN-doh
What's on television?	*¿Qué hay en la televisión?* keh ahy ehn lah teh-leh-bee-see-YOHN

Is it in English or in Spanish?	*¿Está hablado(a) en inglés o en español?* ehs-TAH ah-BLAH-doh (dah) ehn een-GLEHS oh ehn ehs-pah-NYOHL
Has it been dubbed (in English)?	*¿Ha sido doblado(a) (al inglés)?* ah SEE-doh doh-BLAH-doh (dah) (ahl een-GLEHS)
Are there English subtitles?	*¿Hay subtítulos en inglés?* ahy soob-TEE-too-lohs ehn een-GLEHS
What programs are streaming now?	*¿Qué programas se transmiten ahora?* keh proh-GRAH-mahs seh trahns-MEE-tehn ah-OH-rah
I'd like to see …	*Me gustaría ver …* meh goos-tah-REE-yah behr
an adventure film.	*una película de aventura.* OO-nah peh-LEE-koo-lah deh ah-behn-TOO-rah
cartoons.	*dibujos animados.* dee-BOO-hohs ah-nee-MAH-dohs
a comedy.	*una comedia.* OO-nah koh-MEH-dee-yah
a documentary.	*un documental.* oon doh-koo-mehn-TAHL
a drama.	*un drama.* oon DRAH-mah
a game show.	*un juego.* oon HWEH-goh
a horror movie.	*una película de horror.* OO-nah peh-LEE-koo-lah deh oh-RROHR
a love story.	*una película de amor.* OO-nah peh-LEE-koo-lah deh ah-MOHR
a musical.	*una obra musical.* OO-nah OH-brah moo-see-KAHL
a mystery.	*un misterio.* oon mees-TEH-ree-yoh

continues

the news.	*las noticias.* lahs noh-TEE-see-yahs
a police story.	*una película policíaca.* OO-nah peh-LEE-koo-lah poh-lee-see-YAH-kah
a reality show.	*un programa de telerrealidad.* oon proh-GRAH-mah deh teh-leh-rreh-yah-lee-DAHD
a science fiction film.	*una película de ciencia ficción.* OO-nah peh-LEE-koo-lah deh see-YEHN-see-yah feek-see-YOHN
a soap opera.	*una telenovela.* OO-nah teh-leh-noh-BEH- lah
a spy movie.	*una película de espionaje.* OO-nah peh-LEE-koo-lah deh ehs-pee-yoh-NAH-heh
a talk show.	*un programa de entrevistas.* oon proh-GRAH-mah deh ehn-treh-BEES-tahs
the weather.	*el pronóstico meteorológico.* ehl proh-NOHS-tee-koh meh-teh-yoh-roh-LOH-hee- koh
a western.	*una película del oeste (de vaqueros).* OO-nah peh-LEE-koo-lah dehl oh-WEHS-teh (deh bah-KEH-rohs)

Refer to the following explanations when you
choose a movie or theater.

Prohibida para menores de 18 años a menos de que estén acompañados por un adulto.	Forbidden for those under 18 unless accompanied by an adult
Mayores de 13 años.	You must be older than 13.
Versión original.	Original version subtitled

Versión doblada al español.	Dubbed in Spanish
Tarifa reducida.	Reduced rate

Tickets

Excuse me. Could you show me where the ticket office is?	*Disculpe. ¿Me podría indicar dónde queda la taquilla?* dees-KOOL-peh meh poh-DREE-yah een-dee-KAHR DOHN-deh KEH-dah lah tah-KEE-yah
I'd like to pick up my tickets.	*Me gustaría recoger mis entradas.* me goos-tah-REE-yah rreh-koh-HEHR mees ehn-TRAH-dahs
I'd like to purchase tickets for ...	*Me gustaría comprar entradas para ...* meh goos-tah-REE-yah kohm-PRAHR ehn-TRAH-dahs PAH-rah
today.	*hoy.* ohy
this afternoon (evening).	*esta tarde (noche).* EHS-tah TAHR-deh (NOH-cheh)
tomorrow (afternoon) (evening).	*mañana (por la tarde) (por la noche).* mah-NYAH-nah (pohr lah TAHR-deh) (pohr lah NOH-cheh)
Are there seats ... ?	*¿Hay asientos ... ?* ahy ah-see-YEHN-tohs
in the orchestra	*en el patio de butacas* ehn ehl PAH-tee-yoh deh boo-TAH-kahs
in the mezzanine	*en el entrepiso* ehn ehl ehn-treh-PEE-soh
in the balcony	*en el balcón* ehn ehl bahl-KOHN

continues

How much is the ticket?	*¿Cuánto cuesta la entrada?* KWAHN-toh KWEHS-tah lah ehn-TRAH-dah
Are we all sitting together?	*¿Estamos todos sentados juntos?* ehs-TAH-mohs TOH-dohs sehn-TAH-dohs HOON-tohs
Where can I buy a program?	*¿Dónde puedo comprar un programa?* DOHN-deh PWEH-doh kohm-PRAHR oon proh-GRAH-mah

Opinions

It was ...	*Era ...* EH-rah

Positive

awesome.	*genial.* heh-nee-YAHL
excellent.	*excelente.* eh-seh-LEHN-teh
extraordinary.	*extraordinario(a).* ehs-trah-ohr-dee-NAH-ree-yoh (yah)
fabulous.	*fabuloso(a).* fah-boo-LOH-soh (sah)
fantastic.	*fantástico(a).* fahn-TAHS-tee-koh (kah)
fun.	*divertido(a).* dee-behr-TEE-doh (dah)
magnificent.	*magnífico(a).* mahg-NEE-fee-koh (kah)
marvelous.	*maravilloso(a).* mah-rah-bee-YOH-soh (sah)
phenomenal.	*fenomenal.* feh-noh-meh-NAHL
sensational.	*sensacional.* sehn-sah-see-yoh-NAHL

Negative	
boring.	*aburrido(a).* ah-boo-RREE-doh (dah)
horrible.	*horrible.* oh-RREE-bleh
ridiculous.	*ridículo(a).* rree-DEE-koo-loh (lah)
silly.	*tonto (tonta).* TOHN-toh (tah)

Active Sports

I like to ...	*Me gusta ...* meh GOOS-tah
fish.	*pescar.* pehs-KAHR
go hiking.	*hacer senderismo.* ah-SEHR sehn-deh-REES-moh
horseback ride.	*montar a caballo.* mohn-TAHR ah kah-BAH-yoh
parasail.	*hacer parapente.* ah-SEHR pah-rah-PEHN-teh
play golf.	*jugar al golf.* hoo-GAHR ahl gohlf
play soccer.	*jugar al fútbol.* hoo-GAHR ahl FOOT-bohl
play tennis.	*jugar al tenis.* hoo-GAHR ahl TEH-nees
play volleyball.	*jugar al vóleibol.* hoo-GAHR ahl BOH-lehy-bohl
ride a bicycle.	*andar en bicicleta.* ahn-DAHR ehn bee-see-KLEH-tah
sail.	*navegar.* nah-beh-GAHR

continues

scuba dive.	*bucear.* boo-seh-YAHR
skate.	*patinar.* pah-tee-NAHR
ski.	*esquiar.* ehs-kee-YAHR
surf.	*surfear.* soor-feh-YAHR
swim.	*nadar.* nah-DAHR
waterski.	*hacer esquí acuático.* ah-SEHR ehs-KEE ah-KWAH-tee-koh
windsurf.	*hacer windsurf.* ah-SEHR weend-soorf
workout.	*hacer ejercicio.* ah-SEHR eh-hehr-SEE-see-yoh

Venues

Where's the … ?	*¿Dónde está … ?* DOHN-deh ehs-TAH
beach	*la playa* lah PLAH-yah
field	*el campo* ehl KAHM-poh
golf course	*el campo de golf* ehl KAHM-poh deh gohlf
gymnasium	*el gimnasio* ehl heem-NAH-see-yoh
mountain	*la montaña* lah mohn-TAH-nyah
ocean	*el océano* ehl oh-SEH-yah-noh
park	*el parque* ehl PAHR-keh
pool	*la piscina* lah pee-SEE-nah

rink	*la pista* lah PEES-tah
sea	*el mar* ehl mahr
slope (ski)	*la pista (de esquí)* lah PEES-tah (deh ehs-KEE)
tennis court	*la cancha de tenis* lah KAHN-chah deh TEH-nees
track	*la pista* lah PEES-tah

Equipment

We (I) need ...	*Necesitamos (Necesito) ...* neh-seh-see-TAH-mohs (neh-seh-SEE-toh)
Can I borrow ... ?	*¿Me presta ... ?* meh PREHS-tah
(Where) can I rent ... ?	*¿(Dónde) Puedo alquilar ... ?* DOHN-deh (PWEH-doh) ahl-kee-LAHR
(Where) can I buy ... ?	*¿(Dónde) Puedo comprar ... ?* (DOHN-deh) PWEH-doh kohm-PRAHR
an air mattress	*un colchón flotante* oon kohl-CHOHN floh-TAHN-teh
a ball (basketball)	*un balón* oon bah-LOHN
a ball (football, soccer)	*una bola* OO-nah BOH-lah
a beach ball	*una pelota de playa* OO-nah peh-LOH-tah deh PLAH-yah
a beach chair	*un sillón de playa* oon see-YOHN deh PLAH-yah

continues

a beach towel	*una toalla de playa* OO-nah toh-WAH-yah deh PLAH-yah
a beach umbrella	*una sombrilla* OO-nah sohm-BREE-yah
a bicycle	*una bicicleta* OO-nah bee-see-KLEH-tah
a boat	*un barco* oon BAHR-koh
a canoe	*una canoa* OO-nah kah-NOH-wah
a cooler	*una nevera portátil* OO-nah neh-BEH-rah pohr-TAH-teel
diving equipment	*equipo de buceo* eh-KEE-poh deh boo-SEH-yoh
a fishing rod	*una caña de pesca* OO-nah KAH-nyah deh PEHS-kah
golf clubs	*palos de golf* PAH-lohs deh gohlf
a helmet	*un casco* oon KAHS-koh
a racquet	*una raqueta* OO-nah rrah-KEH-tah
skates	*patines* pah-TEE-nehs
skis (water)	*esquís (acuáticos)* ehs-KEES (ah-KWAH-tee-kohs)
sunglasses	*gafas de sol* GAH-fahs deh sohl
suntan lotion	*loción bronceadora* loh-see-YOHN brohn-seh-yah-DOH-rah
a surfboard	*una tabla de surf* OO-nah TAH-blah deh soorf

Spectator Sports

I'd like to see ...	*Me gustaría ver ...* meh goos-tah-REE-yah behr
a bullfight.	*una corrida de toros.* OO-nah koh-RREE-dah deh TOH-rohs
horse races.	*las carreras de caballos.* lahs kah-RREH-rahs deh kah-BAH-yohs
a jai alai match.	*un partido de pelota.* oon pahr-TEE-doh deh peh-LOH-tah
a soccer match.	*un partido de fútbol.* oon pahr-TEE-doh deh FOOT-bohl
Where's the ... ?	*¿Dónde está?* DOHN-deh ehs-TAH
bullring	*la plaza de toros* lah PLAH-sah deh TOH-rohs
the jai alai court	*el frontón* ehl frohn-TOHN
the racetrack	*el hipódromo* ehl ee-POH-droh-moh
the stadium	*el estadio* ehl ehs-TAH-dee-yoh

Nightclubs

What's the cover charge?	*¿Cuánto cuesta la entrada?* KWAHN-toh KWEHS-tah lah ehn-TRAH-dah
Is there a minimum?	*¿Hay un mínimo?* ahy oon MEE-nee-moh?
Is there dancing?	*¿Hay baile?* ahy BAHY-leh
At what time does the show start (end)?	*¿A qué hora empieza (termina) el espectáculo?* ah keh OH-rah ehm-pee-YEH-sah (tehr-MEE-nah) ehl ehs-pehk-TAH-koo-loh

continues

Do I need to show my ID?	*¿Necesito mostrar mi identificación?* neh-seh-SEE-toh mohs-TRAHR mee ee-dehn-tee-fee-kah-see-YOHN
Is a reservation necessary?	*¿Hace falta una reservación?* ah-SEH FAHL-tah OO-nah rreh-sehr-bah-see-YOHN
We'd like a table near the dance floor.	*Nos gustaría una mesa cerca de la pista.* nohs goos-tah-REE-yah OO-nah MEH-sah SEHR-kah deh lah PEES-tah

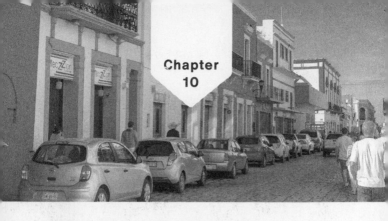

Medical Care

Falling ill when you're away from home is difficult.
The situation becomes even tougher if you can't
communicate what's wrong. This chapter provides
the phrases to explain your ailments and get the
help you need.

Medical Services

I don't feel well.	*No me siento bien.* noh meh see-YEHN-toh bee-YEHN
I've had an accident.	*Tuve un accidente.* TOO-beh oon ahk-see-DEHN-teh
Can you recommend a doctor (specialist) who speaks English?	*¿Puede recomendarme un médico (especialista) de habla inglés?* PWEH-deh rreh-koh-mehn-DAHR-meh oon MEH-dee-koh (ehs-peh-see-yah-LEES-tah deh AH-blah een-GLEHS)
Where's their office?	*¿Dónde está su consultorio?* DOHN-deh ehs-TAH soo kohn-sool-TOH-ree-yoh

Where's the nearest hospital?	*¿Dónde está el hospital más cercano?* DOHN-deh ehs-TAH ehl ohs-pee-TAHL mahs sehr-KAH-noh
How do I get there?	*¿Cómo llegar allí?* KOH-moh yeh-GAHR ah-YEE
Can someone take me there?	*¿Alguien puede llevarme allí?* ahl-gee-YEHN PWEH-deh yeh-bahr-MEH ah-YEE
Please call for an ambulance.	*Por favor llame a una ambulancia.* pohr fah-BOHR YAH-meh ah OO-nah ahm-boo-LAHN-see-yah

Symptoms

My ... hurts.	*Me duele ... .* meh DWEH-leh
ankle	*el tobillo* ehl toh-BEE-yoh
arm (right) (left)	*el brazo (derecho) (izquierdo)* ehl BRAH-soh (deh-REH-choh) (ees-kee-YEHR-doh)
back	*la espalda* lah ehs-PAHL-dah
body	*el cuerpo* ehl KWEHR-poh
chest	*el pecho* ehl PEH-choh
chin	*la barbilla* lah bahr-BEE-yah
ear	*la oreja* lah oh-REH-hah
elbow	*el codo* ehl KOH-doh
eye	*el ojo* ehl OH-hoh

face	*la cara* lah KAH-rah
finger	*el dedo* ehl DEH-doh
foot	*el pie* ehl pee-YEH
forehead	*la frente* lah FREHN-teh
hand	*la mano* lah MAH-noh
head	*la cabeza* lah kah-BEH-sah
hip	*la cadera* lah kah-DEH-rah
knee	*la rodilla* lah rroh-DEE-yah
leg	*la pierna* lah pee-YEHR-nah
lip	*el labio* el LAH-bee-yoh
mouth	*la boca* lah BOH-kah
neck	*el cuello* ehl KWEH-yoh
nose	*la nariz* lah nah-REES
shoulder	*el hombro* ehl OHM-broh
stomach	*el estómago* ehl ehs-TOH-mah-goh
throat	*la garganta* lah gahr-GAHN-tah
toe	*el dedo del pie* ehl DEH-doh dehl pee-YEH
tooth	*el diente* ehl dee-YEHN-teh
wrist	*la muñeca* lah moo-NYEH-kah

continues

I have …	*Tengo …*
	TEHN-goh
a backache.	*dolor de espalda.*
	doh-LOHR deh ehs-PAHL-dah
a blister.	*una ampolla.*
	OO-nah ahm-POH-yah
a bruise.	*una contusión.*
	OO-nah kohn-too-see-YOHN
a burn.	*una quemadura.*
	OO-nah keh-mah-DOO-rah
chills.	*escalofríos.*
	ehs-klah-loh-FREE-yohs
a cold.	*un resfriado.*
	oon rreh-free-YAH-doh
a cough.	*una tos.*
	OO-nah tohs
cramps.	*calambres.*
	kah-LAHM-brehs
a cut.	*un corte.*
	oon KOHR-teh
diarrhea.	*diarrea.*
	dee-yah-RREH-yah
a fever.	*fiebre.*
	fee-YEH-breh
indigestion.	*una indigestión.*
	OO-nah een-dee-hehs-tee-YOHN
a lump.	*un bulto.*
	oon BOOL-toh
a migraine.	*una migraña.*
	OO-nah mee-GRAH-nyah
a rash.	*un sarpullido.*
	oon sahr-poo-YEE-doh
a sore throat.	*un dolor de garganta.*
	oon doh-LOHR deh gahr-GAHN-tah
swelling.	*una hinchazón.*
	OO-nah een-chah-SOHN
a wound.	*una herida.*
	OO-nah eh-REE-dah

I have a cold.	*Tengo un resfriado.* TEHN-goh oon rrehs-free-YAH-doh
I have an earache.	*Me duelen los oídos.* meh DWEH-lehn lohs oy-EE-dohs
I have a stomachache.	*Tengo dolor del estómago.* TEHN-goh doh-LOHR dehl ehs-TOH-mah-goh
I've lost my sense of taste (smell).	*He perdido mi sentido del gusto (olfato).* eh pehr-DEE-doh mee sehn-TEE-doh dehl GOOS-toh (ohl-FAH-toh)
I have a pain in my foot.	*Tengo dolor en el pie.* TEHN-goh doh-LOHR ehn ehl pee-YEH
I feel a (sharp) pain here.	*Siento un dolor agudo aquí.* see-YEHN-toh oon doh-LOHR ah-GOO-doh ah-KEE
Do I have … ?	*¿Tengo … ?* TEHN-goh
a broken bone	*un hueso roto* oon WEH-soh RROH-toh
a fracture	*una fractura* OO-nah frahk-TOO-rah
a sprain	*una torcedura* OO-nah tohr-seh-DOO-rah
I'm bleeding.	*Estoy sangrando.* ehs-TOY sahn-GRAHN-doh
I'm constipated.	*Estoy estreñido(a).* ehs-TOY ehs-treh-NYEE-doh (dah)
I'm coughing.	*Toso.* TOH-soh
I'm dizzy.	*Estoy mareado(a).* ehs-TOY mah-reh-YAH-doh (dah)
I'm exhausted.	*Estoy exhausto(a).* ehs-TOY ehk-SOW-stoh (stah)
I'm nauseous.	*Tengo náuseas.* tehn-GOH NOW-seh-yahs

continues

I'm sneezing.	*Estornudo.* ehs-tohr-NOO-doh
I vomited.	*Vomité.* boh-mee-TEH
I can't sleep.	*No puedo dormir.* noh PWEH-doh dohr-MEER
I can't breathe.	*No puedo respirar.* noh PWEH-doh rrehs-pee-RAHR
I hurt everywhere.	*Me duele todo el cuerpo.* meh DWEH-leh TOH-doh ehl KWEHR-poh
I feel weak.	*Me siento débil.* meh see-YEHN-toh DEH-beel
Do I have coronavirus symptoms?	*¿Tengo síntomas de la enfermedad del coronavirus?* TEHN-goh SEEN-toh-mahs deh lah ehn-fehr-meh-DAHD dehl koh-roh-nah-BEE-roos
I've felt this way since …	*Me he sentido así desde …* meh eh sehn-TEE-doh ah-SEE DEHS-deh
last week.	*la semana pasada.* lah seh-MAH-nah pah-SAH-dah
the day before yesterday.	*anteayer.* ahn-teh-ah-YEHR
yesterday.	*ayer.* ah-YEHR
last night.	*ayer a la noche.* ah-YEHR ah lah NOH-cheh
this morning.	*esta mañana.* ehs-TAH mah-NYAH-nah
this afternoon.	*esta tarde.* EHS-tah TAHR-deh
I fell.	*Me caí.* meh kah-YEE
I fainted.	*Me desmayé.* meh dehs-mah-YEH
I cut myself.	*Me corté.* meh kohr-TEH

I burned myself.	*Me quemé.* meh keh-MEH
An insect bit me.	*Un insecto me picó.* oon een-SEHK-toh meh pee-KOH
A dog bit me.	*Un perro me mordió.* oon PEH-rroh meh mohr-dee-YOH
I'm (not) allergic to …	*(No) soy alérgico(a) …* (noh) soy ah-LEHR-hee-koh (kah)
antibiotics.	*a los antibióticos.* ah lohs ahn-tee-bee-YOH-tee-kohs
anti-inflammatories.	*a los antiinflamatorios.* ah lohs ahn-tee-een-flah-mah-TOH-ree-yohs
bee stings.	*a las picaduras de abeja.* ah lahs pee-kah-DOO-rahs deh ah-BEH-hah
latex.	*al látex.* ahl LAH-tehks
peanuts.	*a los cacahuetes (al maní).* ah lohs kah-kah-HWEH-tehs (ahl mah-NEE)
penicillin.	*a la penicilina.* ah lah peh-nee-see-LEE-nah
pollen.	*al polen.* ahl POH-lehn
shellfish.	*a los mariscos.* ah lohs mah-REES-kohs
I have an adverse reaction to painkillers.	*Tengo una reacción desfavorable a los analgésicos.* TEHN-goh OO-nah rreh-ahk-see-YOHN dehs-fah-boh-RAH-bleh ah lohs ah-nahl-HEH-see-kohs

Medical History

I had … years ago.	*Tuve … hace … años.* TOO-beh … AH-seh … AH-nyohs
back surgery	*cirugía de espalda* see-roo-HEE-yah deh ehs-PAHL-dah
(triple) (quadruple) bypass surgery	*cirurgía de derivación (triple) (quadruple)* see-roo-HEE-yah deh deh-ree-bah-see-YOHN (TREE-pleh) (kwah-DROO-pleh)
cancer	*cáncer* KAHN-sehr
chemotherapy	*quimoterapia* kee-moh-teh-RAH-pee-yah
a heart attack	*un ataque al corazón* oon ah-TAH-keh ahl koh-rah-SOHN
a heart transplant	*un trasplante de corazón* oon trahs-PLAHN-teh deh koh-rah-SOHN
a (right) (left) kidney transplant	*un trasplante de riñon (derecho) (izquierdo)* oon trahs-PLAHN-teh deh ree-NYON (deh-REH-choh) (ees-kee-YEHR-doh)
a liver transplant	*un trasplante de hígado* oon trahs-PLAHN-teh deh EE-gah-doh
radiation	*terapia de radiación* teh-RAH-pee-yah deh rrah-dee-yah-see-YOHN-
a stroke	*una apoplejía* OO-nah ah-poh-pleh-HEE-yah
I have …	*Tengo …* TEHN-goh
AIDS.	*sida.* SEE-dah
cancer.	*cáncer.* KAHN-sehr

Crohn's.	*la enfermedad de Crohn.* lah ehn-fehr-meh-DAHD de krohn
diabetes.	*diabetes.* dee-yah-BEH-tehs
hay fever.	*fiebre del heno.* fee-YEH-breh deh EH-noh
high blood pressure.	*presión arterial alta.* preh-see-YOHN ahr-teh-ree-YAHL AHL-tah
high cholesterol.	*colesterol alto.* oon nee-BEHL deh koh-lehs-teh-ROHL AHL-toh
multiple sclerosis.	*esclerosis múltiple.* ehs-kleh-ROH-sees MOOL-tee-pleh
Parkinson's disease.	*la enfermedad de Parkinson.* lah ehn-fehr-meh-DAHD deh PAHR-keen-sohn
I take these medications: ...	*Tomo estos medicamentos (estas medicinas): ...* TOH-moh EHS-tohs meh-dee-kah-MEHN-tohs (EHS-tahs meh-dee-SEE-nahs)
I'm pregnant.	*Estoy embarazada.* ehs-TOY ehm-bah-rah-SAH-dah
I (don't) smoke.	*(No) Fumo.* (noh) FOO-moh
I (don't) take drugs.	*(No) Tomo drogas.* (noh) TOH-moh DROH-gahs
I (don't) drink alcohol.	*(No) Bebo alcohol.* (noh) BEH-boh ahl-koh-OHL
I had my ... removed.	*Me extrajeron ...* meh ehs-trah-HEH-rohn
appendix	*el apéndice* ehl ah-PEHN-dee-seh
gall bladder	*la vesícula* lah beh-SEE-koo-lah

continues

(right) (left) kidney	*el riñon (derecho)* *(izquierdo)* ehl ree-NYOHN (deh-REH-choh) (ees-kee-YEHR-doh)
(right) (left) lung	*el pulmón (derecho)* *(izquierdo)* ehl pool-MOHN (deh-REH-choh) (ees-kee-YEHR-doh)
spleen	*el bazo* ehl BAH-soh
thyroid	*las tiroides* lahs tee-roh-YEE-dehs
I've had a hysterectomy.	*Tuve una histerectomía.* TOO-beh OO-nah ees-toh-rehk-toh-MEE-yah
I've had the … vaccine (recently).	*Tuve la vacuna …* *recientemente.* TOO-beh lah bah-KOO-nah … rreh-see-yehn-teh-MEHN-teh
diphtheria	*contra la difteria* KOHN-trah lah deef-TEH-ree-yah
flu	*contra la gripe* KOHN-trah lah GREE-peh
hepatitis	*contra la hepatitis* KOHN-trah lah eh-pah-TEE-tees
measles	*contra el sarampión* KOHN-trah ehl sah-rahm-pee-YOHN
MMR	*triple vírica* TREE-pleh BEE-ree-kah
polio	*contra la polio* KOHN-trah lah POH-lee-yoh
pneumonia	*contra la neumonía* KOHN-trah lah neh-yoo-moh-NEE-yah
rubella	*contra la rubéola* KOHN-trah lah rroo-BEH-yoh-lah
shingles	*contra la culebrilla* KOHN-trah lah koo-leh-BREE-yah

tetanus	*contra el tétano* KOHN-trah ehl TEH-tah-noh
typhoid	*contra la fiebre tifoidea* KOHN-trah lah fee-YEH-breh tee-foh-yee-DEH-yah
There's a (no) family history of ...	*(No) hay antecedente de ...* *en mi familia.* (noh) ahy ahn-teh-seh-DEHN-teh deh ... ehn mee fah-MEE-lyah

Diagnosis

What's wrong with me?	*¿Qué tengo?* keh TEHN-goh
Is it serious (contagious)?	*¿Es grave (contagioso)?* ehs GRAH-beh (kohn-tah-hee-YOH-soh
Are you giving me a prescription?	*¿Me da una receta?* meh dah OO-nah rreh-SEH-tah
How many times per day must I take this medicine?	*¿Cuántas veces al día debo tomar este medicamento?* KWAHN-tahs BEH-sehs ahl DEE-yah DEH-boh toh-MAHR EHS-teh meh-dee-kah-MEHN-toh
(How long) Do I have to stay in bed?	*¿(Cuánto tiempo) Tengo que quedarme en la cama?* (KWAHN-toh tee-YEHM-poh) TEHN-goh keh keh-DAHR-meh ehn lah KAH-mah
When can I travel?	*¿Cuándo puedo viajar?* KWAHN-doh PWEH-doh bee-ah-HAHR
How much do I owe you?	*¿Cuánto le debo?* KWAHN-toh leh DEH-boh
May I please have a receipt for my medical insurance?	*¿Por favor podría darme un recibo para mi seguro médico?* pohr fah-BOHR, poh-DREE-yah DAHR-meh oon rreh-SEE-boh PAH-rah mee seh-GOO-roh MEH-dee-koh

At the Pharmacy

A green cross indicates a pharmacy, which sells medication and hygiene, beauty, and baby products.

Where's the nearest (all-night) pharmacy?	*¿Dónde está la farmacia (de guardia) más cercana?* DOHN-deh EHS-tah lah fahr-MAH-see-yah (deh GWAHR-dee-yah) mahs sehr-KAH-nah
Where can I find a compound pharmacy?	*¿Dónde hay una farmacia haciendo preparaciones magistrales?* DOHN-deh ahy OO-nah fahr-MAH-see-yah ah-see-YEHN-doh preh-pah-rah-see-YOH-nehs mah-hee-STRAH-lehs
At what time does it open (close)?	*¿A qué hora abre (cierra)?* ah keh OH-rah AH-breh (see-YEH-rah)
Does this medicine require a prescription?	*¿Este medicamento requiere receta?* EHS-teh meh-dee-kah-MEHN-toh rreh-kee-YEH-reh rreh-SEH-tah
Here it is.	*Aquí la tiene.* ah-KEE lah tee-YEH-neh
Could you please fill this prescription (immediately)?	*¿Por favor podría surtir esta receta (en seguida)?* pohr fah-BOHR, poh-DREE-yah soor-TEER EHS-tah rreh-SEH-tah (ehn seh-GEE-dah)
How long will it take?	*¿Cuánto tiempo tardará?* KWAHN-toh tee-YEHM-poh tahr-dah-RAH
Can I wait here?	*¿Puedo esperar aquí?* PWEH-doh ehs-peh-RAHR ah-KEE
How many pills do I take per day?	*¿Cuántas pastillas tomo por día?* KWAHN-tahs pahs-TEE-yahs TOH-moh pohr DEE-yah
For how many days?	*¿Por cuántos días?* pohr KWAHN-tohs DEE-yahs

How does one take this medicine?	*¿Cómo se toma este medicamento?* KOH-moh seh TOH-mah EHS-teh meh-dee-kah-MEHN-toh
With or without food?	*¿Con o sin comida?* kohn oh seen koh-MEE-dah
Will it make me drowsy?	*¿Me dejará somnoliente?* meh deh-hah-RAH sohm-noh-lee-YEHN-teh
Will it keep me awake?	*¿Me mantendrá despierto(a)?* meh mahn-tehn-DRAH dehs-pee-YEHR-toh (tah)
What are the side effects?	*¿Cuáles son los efectos secundarios?* KWAH-lehs sohn lohs eh-FEHK-tohs seh-koon-DAH-ree-yohs
Are there any contraindications?	*¿Hay contraindicaciones?* ahy kohn-trah-een-dee-kah-see-YOH-nehs
Do you sell the morning-after pill?	*¿Vende la pastilla del día después?* BEHN-deh lah pahs-TEE-yah dehl DEE-yah dehs-PWEHS
I'm looking for …	*Busco …* BOOS-koh
I need …	*Necesito …* neh-seh-SEE-toh
after-shave lotion.	*loción para después de afeitar.* loh-see-YOHN PAH-rah dehs-PWEHS deh ah-feh-yee-TAHR
alcohol.	*alcohol.* ahl-koh-OHL
an antacid.	*un antiácido.* oon ahn-tee-AH-see-doh
an antihistamine.	*un antistamínico.* oon ahn-tee-stah-MEE-nee-koh
an antiseptic.	*un antiséptico.* oon ahn-tee-SEHP-tee-koh

continues

aspirins.	*aspirinas.* ahs-pee-REE-nahs
a bandage.	*una venda.* OO-nah BEHN-dah
Band-Aids.	*curitas.* koo-REE-tahs
blush.	*colorete.* koh-loh-REH-teh
bobby pins.	*pasadores.* pah-sah-DOH-rehs
a bottle (baby).	*un biberón.* oon bee-beh-ROHN
a brush.	*un cepillo.* oon seh-PEE-yoh
cleansing cream.	*limpiador facial.* leem-pee-yah-DOHR fah-see-YAHL
comb.	*un peine.* oon PEHY-neh
condoms.	*condones.* kohn-DOH-nehs
cotton.	*algodón.* ahl-goh-DOHN
cough drops.	*pastillas para la tos.* pahs-TEE-yahs PAH-rah lah tohs
cough syrup.	*jarabe para la tos.* hah-RAH-beh PAH-rah lah tohs
deodorant.	*desodorante.* deh-soh-doh-RAHN-teh
diapers (disposable).	*pañales (desechables).* pah-NYAH-lehs (deh-seh-CHAH-blehs)
ear drops.	*gotas para los oídos.* GOH-tahs PAH-rah lohs oh-YEE-dohs
emery boards.	*limas.* LEE-mahs
eye drops.	*gotas para los ojos.* GOH-tahs PAH-rah lohs OH-hohs

eye shadow.	*sombra de ojos.* SOHM-brah deh OH-hohs
an eyebrow pencil.	*un lápiz de cejas.* oon LAH-pees deh SEH-hahs
an eyeliner.	*un lápiz de ojos.* oon LAH-pees deh OH-hohs
a face mask.	*una mascarilla.* OO-nah mahs-kah-REE-yah
a first-aid kit.	*un botiquín de primeros auxilios.* oon boh-tee-KEEN deh pree-MEH-rohs owk-SEE-lee-yohs
foundation.	*base.* BAH-seh
hairspray.	*laca.* LAH-kah
hand sanitizer.	*gel antiséptico.* hehl ahn-tee-SEHP-tee-koh
hand wipes.	*toallitas antibacterianas.* toh-wah-YEE-tahs ahn-tee-bahk-teh-ree-YAH-nahs
a heating pad.	*una almohadilla de térmica.* OO-nah ahl-moh-ah-DEE-yah deh TEHR-mee-kah
an ice pack.	*una bolsa de hielo.* OO-nah BOHL-sah deh ee-YEH-loh
a laxative (mild).	*un laxante (ligero).* oon lahk-SAHN-teh (lee-HEH-roh)
a lipstick.	*un lápiz de labios.* oon LAH-pees deh LAH-bee-yohs
makeup.	*maquillaje.* mah-kee-YAH-heh
mascara.	*rímel.* RREE-mehl

continues

milk of magnesia.	*leche de magnesia.* LEH-cheh deh mahg-NEH-see-yah
a mirror.	*un espejo.* oon ehs-PEH-hoh
moisturizer.	*crema hidratante.* KREH-mah ee-drah-TAHN-teh
mousse.	*espuma.* ehs-POO-mah
mouthwash.	*enjuague bucal.* ehn-HWAH-geh boo-KAHL
nail clippers.	*un cortauñas.* oon kohr-tah-OO-nyahs
a nail file.	*una lima.* OO-nah LEE-mah
nail polish.	*esmalte.* ehs-MAHL-teh
nail polish remover.	*quitaesmaltes.* kee-tah-ehs-MAHL-tehs
nose drops.	*gotas para la nariz.* GOH-tahs PAH-rah lah nah-REES
a pacifier.	*un chupete.* oon choo-PEH-teh
a razor (disposable).	*una rasuradora (desechable).* OO-nah rah-soo-rah-DOH-rah (deh-seh-CHAH-bleh)
a razor (electric).	*una maquinilla de afeitar (eléctrica).* OO-nah mah-kee-NEE-yah deh ah-feh-yee-TAHR (eh-LEHK-tree-kah) *una rasuradora de afeitar (eléctrica).* [Latin America] OO-nah rrah-soo-rah-DOH-rah deh ah-feh-yee-TAHR (eh-LEHK-tree-kah)

razor blades.	*hojas de afeitar.* OH-hahs deh ah-feh-yee-TAHR
rouge.	*colorete.* koh-loh-REH-teh
safety pins.	*seguros (imperdibles).* seh-GOO-rohs (eem-pehr-DEE-blehs)
sanitary napkins.	*toallas higiénicas.* toh-WAH-yahs ee-hee-YEH-nee-kahs
scissors.	*tijeras.* tee-HEH-rahs
shampoo (anti-dandruff).	*champú (anti-caspa).* chahm-POO (ahn-tee-KAHS-pah)
shaving cream.	*crema de afeitar.* kreh-MAH deh ah-feh-yee-TAHR
sleeping pills.	*pastillas para dormir.* pahs-TEE-yahs PAH-rah dohr-MEER
soap (a bar of).	*jabón (una pastilla de jabón).* hah-BOHN (OO-nah pahs-TEE-yah deh hah-BOHN)
suntan lotion.	*bronceador.* brohn-seh-yah-DOHR
syringes.	*jeringas.* heh-REEN-gahs
tampons.	*tampones.* tahm-POH-nehs
thermometer.	*un termómetro.* oon tehr-MOH-meh-troh
tissues.	*pañuelos de papel.* pah-NYWEH-lohs deh pah-PEHL
a toothbrush.	*un cepillo de dientes.* oon seh-PEE-yoh deh dee-YEHN-tehs
toothpaste.	*pasta dentífrica.* PAHS-tah dehn-TEE-free-kah

continues

tweezers	*pinzas* PEEN-sahs
vitamins.	*vitaminas.* bee-tah-MEE-nahs

At the Dentist

Could you recommend a good dentist?	*¿Podría recomendarme un buen dentista?* poh-DREE-yah rreh-koh-mehn-DAHR-meh oon bwehn dehn-TEES-tah
Where's their office?	*¿Dónde está su consultorio?* DOHN-deh ehs-TAH soo kohn-sool-TOH-ree-yoh
I have a toothache.	*Tengo un dolor de muelas.* TEHN-goh oon doh-LOHR deh MWEH-lahs
I think I have a cavity.	*Creo que tengo una caries.* KREH-yoh keh TEHN-goh OO-nah KAH-ree-yehs
I've broken a tooth.	*Me he roto un diente.* meh eh RROH-toh oon dee-YEHN-teh
My filling fell out.	*Se me cayó el empaste.* seh meh kah-YOH ehl ehm-PAHS-teh
My crown fell off.	*Se me cayó la corona.* seh meh kah-YOH lah koh-ROH-nah
Could you fix it temporarily?	*¿Podría repararlo temporalmente?* poh-DREE-yah rreh-pah-RAHR-loh tehm-poh-rahl-MEHN-teh
Could you fix … ?	*¿Podría reparar … ?* poh-DREE-yah rreh-pah-RAHR
this bridge	*este puente* EHS-teh PWEHN-teh
this crown	*esta corona* EHS-tah koh-ROH-nah
these dentures	*esta dentadura postiza* EHS-tah dehn-tah-DOO-rah pohs-TEE-sah

this implant	*este implante* EHS-teh eem-PLAHN-teh
this tooth	*este diente (muela)* EHS-teh dee-YEHN-teh (MWEH-lah)
Will you have to pull this tooth?	*¿Tendrá que sacar este diente (esta muela)?* tehn-DRAH keh sah-KAHR EHS-teh dee-YEHN-teh (EHS-tah MWEH-lah)
Do I need a root canal?	*¿Necesito un tratamiento de conducto?* neh-seh-SEE-toh oon trah-tah-mee-YEHN-toh deh kohn-DOOK-toh
Is there an infection (an abscess)?	*¿Hay una infección (un absceso)?* ahy OO-nah een-fehk-see-YOHN (oon ahb-SEH-soh)
My gums hurt.	*Me duelen las encías.* meh DWEH-lehn lahs ehn-SEE-yahs
(When) Do I have to come back?	*¿(Cuándo) Debo volver?* (KWAHN-doh) DEH-boh BOHL-behr
How much do I owe you?	*¿Cuánto le debo?* KWAHN-toh leh DEH-boh

Banking, Business & Technology

Conducting business in a foreign country is always a bit of a challenge. It's crucial to know how to exchange money, perform certain banking transactions, arrange business meetings, send a letter, make a phone call, buy stationery items, and deal with modern technology. This chapter will help you with all these tasks.

Banking

Credit and debit cards aren't accepted in all establishments throughout the Spanish-speaking world. You'll also need some cash for small expenses, including taxis, water, and admission fees to some attractions. It's therefore a good idea to exchange some money before your arrival despite the fact you won't get the best rate.

You'll get the best exchange rate if you wait until you arrive. Major airports have a currency exchange desk, but you'll probably get a better rate from an ATM machine affiliated with a major bank.

Una casa de cambio (OO-nah KAH-sah deh KAHM-bee-yoh) also exchanges money.

Some offer terrific rates; others charge exorbitant commissions. It's always a good idea to investigate a few before making a transaction.

Currencies

Country	Currency
Argentina, Chile, Colombia, Cuba, Dominican Republic	*el peso* ehl PEH-soh
Bolivia	*el boliviano* ehl boh-lee-bee-YAH-noh
Costa Rica, El Salvador	*el colón* ehl koh-LOHN
Ecuador	*el sucre* ehl SOO-kreh
Guatemala	*el quetzal* ehl keht-SAHL
Honduras	*el lempira* ehl lehm-PEE-rah
Mexico, Uruguay	*el nuevo peso* ehl NWEH-boh PEH-soh
Nicaragua	*la nueva córdoba* lah NWEH-bah KOHR-doh-bah
Panama	*el balboa* ehl bahl-BOH-wah
Peru	*el nuevo sol* ehl NWEH-boh sohl
Puerto Rico	*el dólar americano* ehl DOH-lahr ah-meh-ree-KAH-noh

| Spain | *el euro*
ehl EH-oo-roh |
| Venezuela | *el bolívar*
ehl boh-LEE-bahr |

Currency Exchange

Where's the nearest money exchange?	*¿Dónde está la casa de cambio más cercana?* DOHN-deh ehs-TAH lah KAH-sah deh KAHM-bee-yoh mahs sehr-KAH-nah
When does it open (close)?	*¿Cuándo abre (cierra)?* KWAHN-doh AH-breh (see-YEH-rah)
Where's the nearest bank?	*¿Dónde está el banco más cercano?* DOHN-deh ehs-TAH ehl BAHN-koh mahs sehr-KAH-noh
What are the banking hours?	*¿Cuál es el horario de atención bancaria?* kwahl ehs ehl oh-RAH-ree-yoh deh ah-tehn-see-YOHN bahn-KAH-ree-yah
What's today's exchange rate for the dollar?	*¿Cuál es la tasa (el tipo) de cambio hoy del dólar?* kwahl ehs lah TAH-sah (ehl TEE-poh) deh KAHM-bee-yoh ohy dehl DOH-lahr
Do you have an automatic teller machine?	*¿Tiene un cajero automático?* tee-YEH-neh oon kah-HEH-roh ow-toh-MAH-tee-koh
Where is it located?	*¿Dónde está?* DOHN-deh ehs-TAH
How does one use it?	*¿Cómo se usa?* KOH-moh seh OO-sah
Is it available all the time?	*¿Está disponible todo el tiempo?* ehs-TAH dees-poh-NEE-bleh TOH-doh ehl tee-YEHM-poh

continues

Can I take my money out 24 hours a day?	*¿Puedo retirar (sacar) mi dinero veinticuatro horas al día?* PWEH-doh rreh-tee-RAHR (sah-KAHR) mee dee-NEH-roh behn-tee-KWAH-troh OH-rahs ahl DEE-yah
Is there a fee for each transaction?	*¿Hay una comisión por cada transacción?* ahy OO-nah koh-mee-see-YOHN pohr KAH-dah trahn-sahk-see-YOHN
How much is it?	*¿Cuànto es?* KWAHN-toh ehs
The ATM ...	*El cajero automático ...* ehl kah-HEH-roh ow-toh-MAH-tee-koh
didn't give me enough money.	*no me dió suficiente dinero.* no meh dee-YOH soo-fee-see-YEHN-teh dee-NEH-roh
gave me too much money.	*me dió demasiado demasiado dinero.* me dee-YOH deh-mah-see-YAH-doh dee-NEH-roh
swallowed my card.	*tragó mi tarjeta.* trah-GOH mee tahr-HEH-tah
Can I cash a personal check?	*¿Puedo cobrar un cheque personal.* PWEHh-doh koh-BRAHR oon CHEH-keh pehr-soh-NAHL
I'd like to change some money.	*Me gustaría cambiar dinero.* meh goos-tah-REE-yah kahm-bee-YAHR dee-NEH-roh
I'd like the money in (large) (small) bills.	*Me gustaría el dinero en billetes (grandes) (pequeños).* meh goos-tah-REE-yah ehl dee-NEH-roh ehn bee-YEH-tehs (GRAHN-dehs) (peh-KEH-nyohs)
Please give me a receipt.	*Por favor déme un recibo.* poh fah-BOHR DEH-meh oon rreh-SEE-boh

I'd like to take a cash advance on my credit card.	*Me gustaría sacar un adelanto en efectivo de mi tarjeta de crédito.* meh goos-tah-REE-yah sah-KAHR oon ah-deh-LAHN-toh ehn eh-fehk-TEE-boh deh mee tahr-HEH-tah deh KREH-dee-toh
I'd like to withdraw money using my debit card.	*Me gustaría retirar dinero usando mi tarjeta de débito.* meh goos-tah-REE-yah rreh-tee-RAHR dee-NEH-roh oo-SAHN-doh mee tahr-HEH-tah deh DEH-bee-toh

Banking Words and Expressions

branch	*la sucursal* lah soo-koor-SAHL
cash	*el dinero en efectivo* ehl dee-NEH-roh ehn eh-fehk-TEE-boh
to cash	*cobrar* koh-BRAHR
cashier	*el cajero* ehl kah-HEH-roh
change (coins)	*la moneda* lah moh-NEH-dah
to change (transaction)	*cambiar* kahm-bee-YAHR
check	*el cheque* ehl CHEH-keh
coin	*la moneda* lah moh-NEH-dah
currency (foreign)	*la moneda extranjera* lah moh-NEH-dah ehs-trahn-HEH-rah
employee	*el empleado (la empleada)* ehl ehm-pleh-YAH-doh (lah ehm-pleh-YAH-dah)
to endorse	*endosar* ehn-doh-SAHR

continues

exchange rate	*la tasa (el tipo) de cambio* lah TAH-sah (ehl TEE-poh) deh KAHM-bee-yoh
to fill out	*llenar* yeh-NAHR
PIN number	*el pin (el número secreto)* *(la clave personal)* ehl peen (ehl NOO-meh-roh seh-KREH-toh) (lah KLAH-beh pehr-soh-NAHL)
receipt	*el recibo* ehl rreh-SEE-boh
to sign	*firmar* feer-MAHR
signature	*la firma* lah FEER-mah
sum	*el total* ehl toh-TAHL
teller	*el cajero (la cajera)* ehl kah-HEH-roh (lah kah-HEH-rah)
void	*inválido(a)* een-BAH-lee-doh (dah)
window	*la ventanilla* lah behn-tah-NEE-yah

Conducting Business

I'm here on business.	*Estoy aquí por negocios.* ehs-TOY ah-KEE pohr neh-GOH-see-yohs
Where's the meeting (conference)?	*¿Dónde está la junta (la conferencia)?* DOHN-deh ehs-TAH lah HOON-tah (lah kohn-feh-REHN-see-yah)
At what time is the (emergency) meeting?	*¿A qué hora es la junta (de emergencia)?* ah keh OH-rah ehs lah HOON-tah (deh eh-mehr-HEHN-see-yah)

The meeting is at 9 a.m. sharp.	*La junta es a las nueve de la mañana en punto.* lah HOON-tah ehs ah lahs NWEH-beh deh lah mah-NYAH-nah ehn POON-toh
Do I need a name tag?	*¿Necesito una etiqueta de nombre?* neh-seh-SEE-toh OO-nah eh-tee-KEH-tah deh NOHM-breh
Where should I sit?	*¿Dónde debería sentarme?* DOHN-deh deh-beh-REE-yah sehn-TAHR-meh
Who's speaking?	*¿Quién habla?* kee-YEHN AH-blah
What topic are we discussing?	*¿Qué tema discutimos?* keh TEH-mah dees-koo-TEE-mohs
I have a meeting (appointment) with …	*Tengo una cita con …* TEHN-goh OO-nah SEE-tah kohn
the auditor.	*el auditor (la auditora).* ehl ow-dee-TOHR (lah ow-dee-TOH-rah)
the bookkeeper (accountant).	*el (la) contable.* ehl (lah) kohn-TAH-bleh *el contador (la contadora)* [Latin America]. ehl kohn-tah-DOHR (lah kohn-tah-DOH-rah)
the CEO.	*el director ejecutivo (la directora ejecutiva).* ehl dee-rehk-TOHR eh-heh-koo-TEE-boh (lah dee-rehk-TOH-rah eh-heh-koo-TEE-bah
the CFO.	*el director financiero (la directora financiera).* ehl dee-rehk-TOHR fee-nahn-see-YEH-roh (lah dee-rehk-TOH-rah fee-nahn-see-YEH-rah)

continues

the COO.	*el director (la directora) de operaciones.* ehl dee-rehk-TOHR (lah dee-rehk-TOH-rah) deh oh-peh-rah-see-YOH-nehs
the head of marketing.	*el jefe (la jefa) de marketing (mercadotecnia).* ehl HEH-feh (lah HEH-fah) deh MAHR-keh-teeng (mehr-kah-doh-TEHK-nee-yah)
the lawyers.	*los abogados (las abogadas).* lohs ah-boh-GAH-dohs (lahs ah-boh-GAH-dahs)
the owner.	*el dueño (la dueña).* ehl DWEH-nyoh (lah DWEH-nyah)
the president.	*el presidente (la presidenta).* ehl preh-see-DEHN-teh (lah preh-see-DEHN-tah)
the vice president.	*el vicepresidente (la vicepresidenta).* ehl bees-preh-see-DEHN-teh (lah bees-preh-see-DEHN-tah)
Where's their office?	*¿Dónde está su oficina?* DOHN-deh ehs-TAH soo oh-fee-SEE-nah
I (don't) need an interpreter.	*(No) Necesito un(a) intérprete.* (noh) neh-seh-SEE-toh oon (OO-nah) een-TEHR-preh-teh
Here's my business card.	*Aquí está mi tarjeta de presentación.* ah-KEE ehs-TAH mee tahr-HEH-tah deh preh-sehn-tah-see-YOHN
Please give me your business card.	*Por favor déme su tarjeta de presentación.* pohr fah-BOHR DEH-meh soo tahr-HEH-tah deh preh-sehn-tah-see-YOHN

I've prepared a PowerPoint presentation.	*He preparado una presentación de PowerPoint.* eh preh-pah-RAH-doh OO-nah preh-sehn-tah-see-YOHN deh PowerPoint.
Please look at the data on this spreadsheet.	*Por favor mire los datos en esta hoja de cálculo.* pohr fah-BOHR MEE-reh lohs DAH-tohs ehn EHS-tah OH-hah deh KAHL-koo-loh
Do you have any questions?	*¿Tiene preguntas?* tee-YEH-neh preh-GOON-tahs
Here's a catalog (price list).	*Aquí hay un catálogo (una lista de precios).* ah-KEE ahy oon kah-TAH-loh-goh (OO-nah LEES-tah deh PREH-see-yohs)
Do you have a catalog of your products?	*¿Tiene un catálogo de sus productos?* tee-YEH-neh oon kah-TAH-loh-goh deh soos proh-DOOK-tohs
Do you have a price list for your products?	*¿Tiene una lista de precios para sus productos?* tee-YEH-neh OO-nah LEES-tah deh PREH-see-yohs PAH-rah soos proh-DOOK-tohs
Can you demonstate how this product works?	*¿Puede demostrar cómo funciona este producto?* PWEH-deh deh-mohs-TRAHR KOH-moh foon-see-YOH-nah EHS-teh proh-DOOK-toh
Marketing strategy is a top priority.	*La estrategia de marketing (mercadotecnia) es de alta prioridad.* lah ehs-trah-TEH-hee-yah deh MAHR-keh-teeng (mehr-kah-doh-TEHK-nee-yah) ehs deh AHL-tah pree-yoh-ree-DAHD
Do you have any (free) marketing materials/ samples)?	*¿Tiene folletos comerciales (gratuitos)?* tee-YEH-neh foh-YEH-tohs koh-mehr-see-yah-LEHS (grah-TWEE-tohs)

continues

Could you give me any (free) samples?	*¿Podría darme muestras (gratuitas)?* poh-DREE-yah DAHR-meh MWEHS-trahs (grah-TWEE-tahs)
Please send me an invoice.	*Por favor envíeme una factura.* pohr fah-BOHR ehn-BEE-yeh-meh OO-nah fahk-TOO-rah
Are the contracts ready?	*¿Están listos los contratos?* ehs-TAHN LEES-tohs lohs kohn-TRAH-tohs
I need to ... my boss.	*Tengo que ... a mi jefe (jefa).* TEHN-goh keh ... ah mee HEH-feh (HEH-fah)
call	*telefonear* teh-leh-foh-neh-YAHR
email	*enviar un correo electrónico* ehn-bee-YAHR oon koh-RREH-yoh eh-lehk-TROH-nee-koh
text	*enviar un mensaje de texto* ehn-bee-YAHR oon mehn-SAH-heh deh TEHKS-toh
We have a permanent (temporary) contract.	*Tenemos un contrato fijo (temporal).* teh-NEH-mohs oon kohn-TRAH-toh FEE-hoh (tehm-poh-RAHL)
Where do I sign?	*¿Dónde tengo que firmar?* DOHN-deh TEHN-goh keh FEER-mahr
We need more time.	*Necesitamos más tiempo.* neh-seh-see-TAH-mohs mahs tee-YEHM-poh

Making a Phone Call

I'll call you soon.	*Le llamaré pronto.* leh yah-mah-REH PROHN-toh
I'll get back to you.	*Me pondré en contacto con Usted.* meh pohn-DREH ehn kohn-TAHK-toh kohn oos-TEHD

What's your (cell) phone number?	*¿Cuál es su número de teléfono (celular) (móvil)?* kwahl ehs soo NOO-meh-roh deh teh-LEH-foh-noh (seh-loo-LAHR) (MOH-beel)
I'll text you.	*Voy a textearle.* boy ah tehks-teh-YAHR-leh
My number is ...	*Mi número es ...* mee NOO-meh-roh ehs
Do you have an answering machine?	*¿Tiene un contestador automático?* tee-YEH-neh oon kohn-tehs-tah-DOHR ow-toh-MAH-tee-koh
May I leave a message?	*¿Puedo dejar un mensaje?* PWEH-doh deh-HAHR oon mehn-SAH-heh
Where's ... ?	*¿Dónde está ... ?* DOHN-deh ehs-TAH
a public phone	*un teléfono público* oon teh-LEH-foh-noh POO-blee-koh
a phone book	*una guía telefónica* OO-nah GEE-yah teh-leh-FOH-nee-kah
May I use your phone?	*¿Puedo usar su teléfono?* PWEH-doh OO-sahr soo teh-LEH-foh-noh
Where can I buy ... ?	*¿Dónde puedo comprar ... ?* DOHN-deh PWEH-doh kohm-PRAHR
a prepaid phone card	*una tarjeta telefónica prepagada* OO-nah tahr-HEH-tah teh-leh-FOH-nee-kah preh-pah-GAH-dah
a prepaid cell phone	*un celular (móvil, [Spain]) prepagado* oon seh-loo-LAHR (MOH-beel) preh-pah-GAH-doh

continues

Do you have a cell phone charger?	*¿Tiene un cargador de celular (móvil)?* tee-YEH-neh oon kahr-gah-DOHR deh seh-loo-LAHR (MOH-beel)
May I borrow it?	*¿Me lo presta?* meh loh PREHS-tah
May I use it?	*¿Puedo usarlo?* PWEH-doh OO-sahr-loh
Hello. This is …	*Hola. Habla …* OH-lah AH-blah
May I speak to … ?	*¿Puedo hablar con … ?* PWEH-doh ah-BLAHR kohn
Please speak louder (slower).	*Por favor hable más alto (despacio).* pohr fah-BOHR AH-bleh mahs AHL-toh (dehs-PAH-see-yoh)
Don't hang up.	*No cuelgue.* noh KWEHL-geh
Sorry, I have the wrong number.	*Lo siento, tengo un número equivocado.* loh see-YEHN-toh TEHN-goh oon NOO-meh-roh eh-kee-boh-KAH-doh
We got cut off (disconnected).	*Se nos cortó la línea.* seh nohs kohr-TOH lah LEE-neh-yah
There's a lot of static on the line.	*Hay mucha estática en la línea.* ahy MOO-chah ehs-TAH-tee-kah ehn lah LEE-neh-yah
I can't hear.	*No puedo oír.* noh PWEH-doh oy-EER
Can you hear me now?	*Puede(s) oírme?* PWEH-deh(s) oy-EER-meh
I have to charge my phone.	*Tengo que recargar mi celular (móvil).* TEHN-goh keh rreh-kahr-GAHR mee seh-loo-LAHR (MOH-beel)
Where can I do it?	*¿Dónde puedo hacerlo?* DOHN-deh PWEH-doh ah-SEHR-loh

I'll call you back.	*Le llamaré.* leh yah-mah-REH

Business Words and Expressions

accountant	*el contador (la contadora)* ehl kohn-tah-DOHR (lah kohn-tah-DOH-rah)
assets	*el activo* ehl ahk-TEE-boh
authorize	*autorizar* ow-toh-ree-SAHR
a bargain	*una ganga* OO-nah GAHN-gah
bill	*la factura* lah fahk-TOO-rah
bill of sale	*el contrato de venta* ehl kohn-TRAH-toh deh BEHN-tah
bookkeeping	*la contabilidad* lah kohn-tah-bee-lee-DAHD
business	*los negocios* lohs neh-GOH-see-yohs
buy	*comprar* kohm-PRAHR
buy at auction	*comprar en subasta* kohm-PRAHR ehn soo-BAHS-tah
buy for cash	*pagar al contado* pah-GAHR ahl kohn-TAH-doh
buy on credit	*comprar a crédito* kohm-PRAHR ah KREH-dee-toh
a buyout	*una adquisición* OO-nah ahd-kee-see-see-YOHN
to buy out (take over ownership)	*comprar la parte* kohm-PRAHR lah PAHR-teh
cash a check	*cobrar un cheque* koh-BRAHR oon CHEH-keh

continues

competitive price	*el precio competidor* ehl PREH-see-yoh kohm-peh-tee-DOHR
consumer	*el consumidor* ehl kohn-soo-mee-DOHR
contract	*el contrato* ehl kohn-TRAH-toh
credit	*el crédito* ehl KREH-dee-toh
debit	*el débito* ehl DEH-bee-toh
deliver	*entregar* ehn-treh-GAHR
discount	*el descuento* ehl dehs-KWEHN-toh
expenses	*los gastos* lohs GAHS-tohs
export	*exportar* ehs-pohr-TAHR
foreign trade	*el comercio exterior* ehl koh-MEHR-see-yoh ehs-teh-ree-YOHR
goods	*los productos* lohs proh-DOOK-tohs
import	*importar* eem-pohr-TAHR
interest rate	*la tasa (el tipo) de interés* lah TAH-sah (ehl TEE-poh) deh een-teh-REHS
invoice	*la factura* lah fahk-TOO-rah
management	*la gestión* lah hehs-tee-YOHN
manager	*el director (la directora)* ehl dee-rehk-TOHR (lah dee-rehk-TOH-rah)
merchandise	*la mercancía* lah mehr-kahn-SEE-yah
money	*el dinero* ehl dee-NEH-roh
office	*la oficina* lah oh-fee-SEE-nah

overhead expenses	*los gastos generales* lohs GAHS-tohs heh-neh-RAH-lehs
owner	*el dueño (la dueña)* ehl DWEH-nyoh (lah DWEH-nyah)
package	*el paquete* ehl pah-KEH-teh
partner	*el socio* ehl SOH-see-yoh
payment	*el pago* ehl PAH-goh
producer	*el productor* ehl proh-dook-TOHR
property	*la propiedad* lah proh-pee-yeh-DAHD
purchase	*la compra* lah KOHM-prah
retailer	*el minorista* ehl mee-noh-REES-tah
sale	*la venta* lah BEHN-tah
sample	*la muestra* lah MWEHS-trah
selling price	*el precio de venta* ehl PREH-see-yoh deh BEHN-tah
send	*mandar* mahn-DAHR
send back	*devolver* deh-bohl-BEHR
send C.O.D. (cash on delivery)	*mandar contra reembolso* mahn-DAHR KOHN-trah rreh-ehm-BOHL-soh
settle	*arreglar* ah-rreh-GLAHR
shipment	*el envío* ehl ehn-BEE-yoh
tax	*el impuesto* ehl eem-PWEHS-toh

continues

tax-exempt	*libre de impuestos* LEE-breh deh eem-PWEHS-tohs
trade	*el comercio* ehl koh-MEHR-see-yoh
transact business	*hacer negocios* ah-SEHR neh-GOH-see-yohs
value-added tax	*el impuesto sobre el valor añadido* ehl eem-PWEHS-toh SOH-breh ehl bah-LOHR ah-nyah-DEE-doh
wholesaler	*el mayorista* ehl mah-yoh-REES-tah

At the Post Office

Where's the nearest post office?	*¿Dónde está la oficina de correos más cercana?* DOHN-deh ehs-TAH lah oh-fee-SEE-nah deh koh-RREH-yohs mahs sehr-KAH-nah
Where's the nearest mailbox?	*¿Dónde está el buzón más cercano?* DOHN-deh ehs-TAH ehl boo-SOHN mahs sehr-kah-NOH
Where can I buy stamps (a phone card)?	*¿Dónde puedo comprar sellos (una tarjeta telefónica)?* DOHN-deh PWEH-doh kohm-PRAHR SEH-yohs (OO-nah tahr-HEH-tah teh-leh-FOH-nee-kah)
What's the postage rate for ... ?	*¿Cuál es la tarifa de franqueo de ... ?* kwahl ehs lah tah-REE-fah deh frahn-KEH-yoh deh
a letter (to the United States)	*una carta (a los Estados Unidos)* OO-nah KAHR-tah ah lohs ehs-TAH-dohs OO-nee-dohs
a package	*un paquete postal* oon pah-KEH-teh pohs-TAHL

a postcard	*una postal* OO-nah pohs-TAHL
a registered letter	*una carta certificada* OO-nah KAHR-tah sehr- tee-fee-KAH-dah
a special-delivery letter	*una carta urgente* OO-nah KAHR-tah oor- HEHN-teh
How much does this letter (package) weigh?	*¿Cuánto pesa esta carta (este paquete)?* KWAHN-toh PEH-sah EHS-tah KAHR-tah (EHS-teh pah-KEH-teh)
This package is fragile.	*Este paquete es frágil.* EHS-teh pah-KEH-teh ehs FRAH-heel
When will it arrive?	*¿Cuándo llegará?* KWAHN-doh yeh-gah-RAH
Do I have to fill out a custom's declaration?	*¿Debo completar una declaración de aduana?* DEH-boh kohm-pleh-TAHR OO-nah deh-klah-rah-see-YOHN deh ah-DWAH-nah

Office Supplies

I need to buy …	*Tengo que comprar …* TEHN-goh keh kohm-PRAHR
a ballpoint pen.	*un bolígrafo.* oon boh-LEE-grah-foh
a calculator.	*una calculadora.* OO-nah kahl-koo-lah-DOH-rah
envelopes.	*sobres.* SOH-brehs
an eraser.	*una goma.* OO-nah GOH-mah
glue.	*pegamento.* peh-gah-MEHN-toh
a notebook.	*un cuaderno.* oon kwah-DEHR-noh

continues

paper.	*papel.*
	pah-PEHL
paper clips.	*clips.*
	kleeps
pencils.	*lápices.*
	LAH-pee-sehs
a pencil sharpener.	*un sacapuntas.*
	oon sah-kah-POON-tahs
Post-its.	*notas post-it.*
	NOH-tahs POHST-eet
a ruler.	*una regla.*
	OO-nah RREH-glah
scotch tape.	*cinta adhesiva.*
	SEEN-tah ahd-eh-SEE-bah
a stapler.	*una grapadora.*
	OO-nah grah-pah-DOH-rah
wrapping paper.	*papel para regalo.*
	pah-PEHL PAH-rah rreh-GAH-loh
a writing pad.	*un bloc.*
	oon blohk

Faxes, Emails, and Texts

Do you have a fax machine?	*¿Tiene un fax?*
	tee-YEH-neh oon fahks
What's your fax (cell phone) number?	*¿Cuál es su número de fax (celular, móvil)?*
	kwahl ehs soo NOO-meh-roh deh fahks (seh-loo-LAHR, MOH-beel)
What's your email address?	*¿Cuál es su dirección de correo electrónico?*
	kwahl ehs soo dee-rehk-see-YOHN deh koh-RREH-yoh eh-lehk-TROH-nee-koh
I'd like to send ...	*Me gustaría mandar ...*
	meh goos-tah-REE-yah mahn-DAHR
a fax.	*un fax.*
	oon fahks

a text.	*un mensaje de texto.* oon mehn-SAH-heh deh TEHKS-toh
an email.	*un correo electrónico.* oon koh-RREH-yoh eh-lehk-TROH-nee-koh
May I send ... this to you?	*¿Puedo enviarle esto por ... ?* PWEH-doh ehn-bee-YAHR-leh EHS-toh pohr
email	*correo electrónico* koh-RREH-yoh eh-lehk-TROH-nee-koh
fax	*fax* fahks
text	*mensaje de texto* mehn-SAH-heh deh TEHKS-toh
... it to me.	*Envíeemelo por ...* ehn-BEE-yeh-meh-loh pohr
Email	*correo electrónico.* koh-RREH-yoh eh-lehk-TROH-nee-koh
Fax	*fax.* fahks
Text	*mensaje de texto.* mehn-SAH-heh deh TEHKS-toh
I didn't get your ...	*Yo no recibí su ...* yoh noh rreh-see-BEE soo
email.	*correo electrónico.* koh-RREH-yoh eh-lehk-TROH-nee-koh
fax.	*fax.* fahks
text.	*mensaje de texto.* mehn-SAH-heh deh TEHKS-toh
Did you receive my ... ?	*¿Recibió mi ... ?* rreh-see-bee-YOH mee
email	*correo electrónico* koh-RREH-yoh eh-lehk-TROH-nee-koh

continues

fax	*fax* fahks
text	*mensaje de texto* mehn-SAH-heh deh TEHKS-toh

Photocopies

I'd like to make a photocopy of this paper (document).	*Me gustaría hacer una fotocopia de este papel (documento).* meh goos-tah-REE-yah ah-SEHR OO-nah foh-toh-KOH-pee-yah deh EHS-teh pah-PEHL (doh-koo-MEHN-toh)
I'd like to have a photocopy made.	*Me gustaría mandar hacer una fotocopia.* meh goos-tah-REE-yah mahn-DAHR ah-SEHR OO-nah foh-toh-KOH-pee-yah
What's the cost per page?	*¿Cuánto cuesta por página?* KWAHN-toh KWEHS-tah pohr PAH-hee-nah
Can you enlarge it (by 50 percent)?	*¿Puede agrandarlo (cincuenta por ciento)?* PWEH-deh ah-grahn-DAHR-loh (seen-KWEHN-tah pohr see-YEHN-toh)
Can you reduce it (by 25 percent)?	*¿Puede reducirlo (veinticinco por ciento)?* PWEH-deh rreh-doo-SEER-loh (behyn-tee-SEEN-koh pohr see-YEHN-toh)
Can you make a color copy?	*¿Puede hacer una copia en color?* PWEH-deh ah-SEHR OO-nah KOH-pee-yah ehn koh-LOHR

Computers

I have to use a computer.	*Debo usar una computadora (un ordenador* [Spain]*).* DEH-boh OO-sahr OO-nah kohm-poo-tah-DOH-rah (oon ohr-deh-nah-DOHR)
Do you have a Mac or a PC?	*¿Tiene una Mac o una PC?* tee-YEH-neh OO-nah Mac oh OO-nah peh-SEH
Do you have a laptop (wireless)?	*¿Tiene un portátil (inalámbrico)?* tee-YEH-neh oon pohr-TAH-teel (ee-nah-LAHM-bree-koh)
May I use this computer?	*¿Puedo usar esta computadora?* PWEH-doh OO-sahr EHS-tah kohm-poo-tah-DOH-rah
Is it available?	*¿Está disponible?* esh-TAH dees-poh-NEE-bleh
Does it have antivirus software?	*¿Tiene un programa antivirus?* tee-YEH-neh oon proh-GRAH-mah ahn-tee-BEE-roos
How can I connect to the Internet?	*¿Cómo puedo conectarme a la red?* KOH-moh PWEH-doh koh-nehk-TAHR-meh ah lah rrehd
I need a wireless Internet connection.	*Necesito una conexión inalámbrica.* neh-seh-SEE-toh OO-nah koh-nehk-see-YOHN ee-nah-LAHM-bree-kah
Do you have wireless access?	*¿Tiene acceso inalámbrico?* tee-YEH-neh ahk-SEH-soh ee-nah-LAHM-bree-koh
Is there (free) Wi-Fi access here?	*¿Hay acceso Wi-Fi gratuito aquí?* ahy ahk-SEH-soh Wi-Fi grah-TWEE-toh ah-KEE

continues

What's the Wi-Fi password?	*¿Cuál es la contraseña de Wi-Fi?* kwahl ehs lah kohn-trah-SEH-nyah de Wi-Fi
What search engine should I use?	*¿Qué buscador debo usar?* keh boos-kah-DOHR DEH-boh OO-sahr
Which websites will help me?	*¿Qué sitios web me ayudarán?* keh SEE-tee-yohs wehb meh ah-yoo-dah-RAHN
What's your e-mail address?	*¿Cuál es su dirección de correo electrónico?* kwahl ehs soo dee-rehk-see-YOHN deh koh-RREH-yoh eh-lehk-TROH-nee-koh
What's your website?	*¿Cuál es su sitio web?* kwahl ehs soo SEE-tee-yoh wehb
Can you help me? This link isn't working.	*¿Puede ayudarme? Este enlace no funciona.* PWEH-deh ah-yoo-DAHR-meh EHS-teh ehn-LAH-seh noh foon-see-YOH-nah
Where's the nearest Internet café (hotspot)?	*¿Dónde está el hotspot (el lugar con red inalámbrica) más cercano?* DOHN-deh ehs-TAH ehl hotspot (ehl loo-GAHR kohn rrehd ee-nah-LAHM-bree-kah) mahs sehr-KAH-noh
Where can I find a listing of hotspots?	*¿Dónde puedo encontrar una guía de hotspots?* DOHN-deh PWEH-doh ehn-kohn-TRAHR OO-nah GEE-yah deh hotspots
How can I activate (buy) an online Wi-Fi account?	*¿Cómo puedo activar (comprar) una cuenta en línea Wi-Fi?* KOH-moh PWEH-doh ahk-tee-BAHR (kohm-PRAHR) OO-nah KWEHN-tah ehn LEE-neh-yah Wi-Fi
My computer crashed.	*Mi computadora se colgó.* mee kohm-poo-tah-DOH-rah seh kohl-GOH

My computer isn't working.	*Mi computadora no funciona.* mee kohm-poo-tah-DOH-rah noh foon-see-YOH-nah
Where can I get it fixed?	*¿Dónde puedo arreglarlo?* DOHN-deh PWEH-doh ah-rreh-GLAHR-loh
Is it possible to print this from here?	*¿Es posible imprimir esto desde aquí?* ehs poh-SEE-bleh eem-pree-MEER EHS-toh DEHS-deh ah-KEE
Please scan and send this.	*Por favor escanee y envíe esto.* pohr fah-BOHR ehs-kah-neh-EH ee ehn-BEE-yeh EHS-toh
The printer is running out of ink.	*A la impresora se le está acabando la tinta.* ah lah eem-preh-SOH-rah seh leh ehs-TAH ah-kah-BAHN-doh lah TEEN-tah
The printer ran out of ink.	*La impresora se quedó sin tinta.* lah eem-preh-SOH-rah seh KEH-doh seen TEEN-tah
Can you help me? There's a paper jam.	*¿Puede ayudarme? Hay un atasco de papel.* PWEH-deh ah-yoo-DAHR-meh ahy oon ah-TAHS-koh deh pah-PEHL
Where can I print my boarding pass?	*¿Dónde puedo imprimir mi tarjeta de embarque?* DOHN-deh PWEH-doh eem-pree-MEER mee tahr-HEH-tah deh ehm-BAHR-keh

Computer Words and Expressions

access	*el acceso* ehl ahk-SEH-soh
antivirus software	*un programa antivirus* oon proh-GRAH-mah ahn-tee-BEE-roos

continues

app	*una aplicación* OO-nah ah-plee-kah-see-YOHN
to attach	*adjuntar* ahd-hoon-TAHR
attachment	*el adjunto* ehl ahd-HOON-toh
backup	*hacer un respaldo* ah-SEHR oon rrehs-pahl-DOH
blog	*el blog* ehl blohg
bookmark	*el favorito* ehl fah-boh-REE-toh
to bookmark	*marcar* mahr-KAHR
to boot up	*iniciar* ee-nee-see-YAHR
browser	*el navegador* ehl nah-beh-gah-DOHR
cartridge	*el cartucho* ehl kahr-TOO-choh
to click	*hacer clic* ah-SEHR kleek
clipboard	*el portapapeles* ehl pohr-tah-pah-PEH-lehs
computer	*la computadora* [Latin America], *el ordenador* [Spain] lah kohm-poo-tah-DOH-rah, ehl ohr-deh-nah-DOHR
computer science	*la informática* lah een-fohr-MAH-tee-kah
to copy	*copiar* koh-pee-YAHR
connection	*la conexión* lah koh-nehk-see-YOHN
cursor	*el cursor* ehl KOOR-sohr
to cut	*cortar* kohr-TAHR
desktop	*el escritorio* ehl ehs-kree-TOH-ree-yoh

database	*la base de datos* lah BAH-seh deh DAH-tohs
to delete	*borrar* boh-RRAHR
document	*el documento* ehl doh-koo-MEHN-toh
to download	*descargar* dehs-kahr-GAHR
to drag	*arrastrar* ah-rrahs-TRAHR
email	*el correo electrónico* ehl koh-RREH-yoh eh-lehk-TROH-nee-koh
file	*el archivo* ehl ahr-CHEE-boh
firewall	*el cortafuegos* ehl kohr-tah-FWEH-gohs
folder	*la carpeta* lah kahr-PEH-tah
function key	*la tecla de función* lah TEH-klah deh foon-see-YOHN
graphics	*los gráficos* lohs GRAH-fee-kohs
hacker	*el/la pirata* ehl/lah pee-RAH-tah
home page	*la página principal* lah PAH-hee-nah preen-see-PAHL
icon	*el ícono* ehl EE-koh-noh
ink	*la tinta* lah TEEN-tah
to insert	*insertar* een-sehr-TAHR
Internet café	*el cibercafé* ehl see-behr-kah-FEH
junk mail	*el correo basura* ehl koh-RREH-yoh bah-SOO-rah
key	*la tecla* lah TEH-klah

continues

keyboard	*el teclado* ehl TEH-klah-doh
laptop computer	*el portátil* ehl pohr-TAH-teel
line	*la linéa* lah lee-NEH-yah
link	*el enlace* ehl ehn-LAH-seh
memory	*la memoria* lah meh-MOH-ree-yah
to merge	*fusionar* foo-see-yoh-NAHR
message	*el mensaje* ehl mehn-SAH-heh
modem	*el módem* ehl MOH-dehm
monitor	*el monitor, la pantalla* ehl moh-nee-TOHR, lah pahn-TAH-yah
mouse	*el ratón* ehl rrah-TOHN
network	*la red* lah rrehd
password	*la contraseña* lah kohn-trah-SEH-nyah
to paste	*pegar* peh-GAHR
to print	*imprimir* eem-pree-MEER
printer	*la impresora* lah eem-preh-SOH-rah
program	*el programa* ehls proh-GRAH-mah
public domain	*el dominio público* ehl doh-MEE-nee-yoh POO-blee-koh
to reboot	*reiniciar* rreh-ee-nee-see-YAHR
to save	*guardar* gwahr-DAHR

to scan	*escanear* ehs-kah-neh-YAHR
screen	*la pantalla* lah pahn-TAH-yah
search engine	*el buscador* ehl boos-kah-DOHR
server	*el servidor* ehl sehr-bee-DOHR
shortcut (keyboard)	*el atajo* ehl ah-TAH-hoh
site	*el sitio* ehl SEE-tee-yoh
software	*el software* ehl SOHFT-wehr
spam	*el correo basura* ehl koh-RREH-yoh bah-SOO-rah
spell-checker	*el verificador de ortografía* ehl beh-ree-fee-kah-DOHR deh ohr-toh-grah-FEE-yah
spreadsheet	*la hoja de cálculo* lah OH-hah deh KAHL-koo-loh
symbol	*el símbolo* ehl SEEM-boh-loh
thesaurus	*el tesauro* ehl teh-SOW-roh
thread	*el hilo* ehl EE-loh
thumb drive	*la memoria flash* lah meh-MOH-ree-yah flahsh
touchscreen	*la pantalla táctil* lah pahn-TAH-yah TAHK-teel
to turn off	*apagar* ah-pah-GAHR
to turn on	*encender* ehn-sehn-DEHR
tweet	*el tweet* ehl tweet
Twitter	*el twitter* ehl TWEE-tehr

continues

window	*la ventana*
	lah behn-TAH-nah
word processor	*el procesador de texto*
	ehl proh-seh-sah-DOHR deh
	TEHKS-toh

English
to Spanish
Dictionary

a, an *un, uno, una* [oon, OO-noh, OO-nah]

able (to be able) *poder* [poh-DEHR]

about *de, a eso de* [deh, ah EH-soh deh]

above *encima de* [ehn-SEE-mah deh]

to have an ache (in) *tener dolor (de)* [teh-NEHR doh-LOHR (deh)]

to accompany *acompañar* [ah-kohm-pah-NYAHR]

address *dirección* (f.) [dee-rehk-see-YOHN]

to adjust *arreglar* [ah-RREH-glahr]

after *después (de)* [dehs-PWEHS (deh)]

afternoon *tarde* (f.) [TAHR-deh]

again *de nuevo* [deh NWEH-boh]

against *contra* [KOHN-trah]

ago *hace + period of time* [AH-seh]

air-conditioning *aire* (m.) *acondicionado* [AHY-reh ah-kohn-dee-see-yoh-NAH-doh]

airline *aerolínea* (f.) [ahy-roh-LEE-neh-yah]

airport *aeropuerto* (m.) [ahy-roh-PWEHR-toh]

all *todo(a)* [TOH-doh (dah)]

allergic *alérgico(a)* [ah-LEHR-hee-koh (kah)]

almost *casi* [KAH-see]

already *ya* [yah]

also *también* [tahm-bee-YEHN]

always *siempre* [see-YEHM-preh]

American consulate *consulado* (m.) *americano* [kohn-soo-LAH-doh] [ah-meh-ree-KAH-noh]

American embassy *embajada* (f.) *americana* [ehm-bah-HAH-dah] [ah-meh-ree-KAH-nah]

among *entre* [EHN-treh]

another *otro(a)* [OH-troh (trah)]

apple *manzana* (f.) [mahn-SAH-nah]

appointment *cita* (f.) [SEE-tah]

April *abril* [AH-breel]

arm *brazo* (m.) [BRAH-soh]

around *alrededor (de)* [ahl-reh-deh-DOHR]

to arrive *llegar* [yeh-GAHR]

ashtray *cenicero* (m.) [seh-nee-SEH-roh]

to ask *preguntar, pedir* [preh-goon-TAHR, peh-DEER]

aspirins *aspirinas* (f. pl.) [ahs-pee-REE-nahs]

at *a* [ah]

ATM *cajero* (m.) *automático* [kah-HEH-roh ow-toh-MAH-] [tee-koh]

August *agosto* [ah-GOHS-toh]

autumn *otoño* (m.) [oh-TOH-nyoh]

available *disponible* [dees-poh-NEE-bleh]

bad *malo(a)* [MAH-loh (lah)]

bag *bolsa* (f.) [BOHL-sah]

bakery *panadería* (f.) [pah-nah-deh-REE-yah]

ballpoint pen *bolígrafo* (m.) [boh-LEE-grah-foh]

banana *banana* (f.) [bah-NAH-nah]

Band-Aid *curita* (f.) [koo-REE-tah]

bank *banco* (m.) [BAHN-koh]

bathing suit *traje* (m.) *de baño* [trah-HEH deh BAH-nyoh]

bathroom *baño(s)* (m. [pl.]), *servicios* (m. pl.) [BAH-nyoh(s), sehr-BEE-see-yohs]

to be *estar, ser* [ehs-TAHR, sehr]

beach *playa* (f.) [PLAH-yah]

because *porque* [POHR-keh]

beef *carne* (f.) *de vaca* [KAHR-neh deh BAH-kah]

beer *cerveza* (f.) [sehr-BEH-sah]

before *antes (de)* [AHN-tehs (deh)]

to begin *comenzar, empezar* [koh-mehn-SAHR, ehm-peh-SAHR]

behind *detrás (de)* [deh-TRAHS (deh)]

bellman *botones* (m.) [boh-TOH-nehs]

below, beneath *debajo de* [deh-BAH-hoh deh]

between *entre* [EHN-treh]

big *grande* [GRAHN-deh]

bill (commerce) *factura* (f.) [fahk-TOO-rah]

bill (money) *billete* (m.) [bee-YEH-teh]

bill (restaurant) *cuenta* (f.) [(KWEHN-tah)]

black *negro(a)* [NEH-groh (grah)]

blanket *manta* (f.) [MAHN-tah]

block (street) *cuadra* (f.) [KWAH-drah]

blouse *blusa* (f.) [BLOO-sah]

blue *azul* [ah-SOOL]

to board *abordar* [ah-bohr-DAHR]

boarding pass *tarjeta* (f.) *de embarque* [tahr-HEH-tah deh ehm-BAHR-keh]

boat *barco* (m.) [BAHR-koh]

book *libro* (m.) [LEE-broh]

bookstore *librería* (f.) [lee-breh-REE-yah]

boots *botas* (f. pl.) [BOH-tahs]

to borrow *usar, pedir prestado* [OO-sahr, peh-DEER prehs-TAH-doh]

bottle *botella* (f.) [boh-TEH-yah]

box *caja* (f.) [KAH-hah]

brand name *marca* (f.) [MAR-kah]

bread *pan* (m.) [pahn]

to bring *traer* [trah-YEHR]

brother *hermano* (m.) [ehr-MAH-noh]

brown *marrón, pardo (parda)* [mah-RROHN, PAHR-doh (dah)]

bus *autobús* (m.) [ow-toh-BOOS]

bus stop *parada* (f.) *de autobús* [pah-RAH-dah deh ow-toh-BOOS]

business card *tarjeta* (f.) *de presentación* [tahr-HEH-tah deh preh-sehn-tah-see-YOHN]

butcher shop *carnicería* (f.)
[kahr-nee-seh-REE-yah]

butter *mantequilla* (f.)
[mahn-teh-KEE-yah]

to buy *comprar* [kohm-PRAHR]

by *por* [pohr]

cake *pastel* (m.) [pahs-TEHL]

calculator *calculadora* (f.)
[kahl-koo-lah-DOH-rah]

to call *telefonear, llamar*
[teh-leh-foh-neh-YAHR, yah-MAHR]

can *lata* (f.) [LAH-tah]

can (to be able to)
poder [poh-DEHR]

candy *dulces* (m. pl.)
[DOOL-sehs]

candy store *dulcería* (f.)
[dool-seh-REE-yah]

car *coche* (m.), *automóvil*
(m.), *carro* (m.) [KOH-cheh,
ow-toh-MOH-beel, KAH-rroh]

cash *dinero* (m.) [dee-NEH-roh]

cash advance *adelanto* (m.)
en efectivo [ah-deh-LAHN-toh
ehn] [eh-fehk-TEE-boh]

to cash (a check) *cobrar
un cheque* [koh-BRAHR oon
CHEH-keh]

cashier *cajero(a)* [kah-HEH-roh (rah)]

cat *gato* (m.) [GAH-toh]

cell phone *celular* (m.) *móvil*
(m.)[Latin America] [seh-
loo-LAHR teh-LEH-foh-noh
MOH-beel]

chair *silla* (f.) [SEE-yah]

change (coins) *moneda* (f.)
[moh-NEH-dah]

to change *cambiar* [kahm-bee-YAHR]

check *cheque* (m.) [CHEH-keh]

cheese *queso* (m.) [KEH-soh]

cherry *cereza* (f.) [seh-REH-sah]

chicken *pollo* (m.) [POH-yoh]

church *iglesia* (f.) [ee-GLEH-see-yah]

clean *limpio(a)* [LEEM-pee-yoh (yah)]

clock *reloj* (m.) [rreh-LOH]

to close *cerrar* [seh-RAHR]

clothing store *tienda* (f.)
de ropa [tee-YEHN-dah deh
RROH-pah]

coffee *café* (m.) [kah-FEH]

cold, to be cold (person)
tener frío [teh-NEHR FREE-yoh]

cold, to be cold (weather)
hacer frío [ah-SEHR FREE-yoh]

color *color* (m.) [koh-LOHR]

to come *venir* [beh-NEER]

computer *computadora* (f.)
[Latin America] [kohm-poo-
tah-DOH-rah], *ordenador* (m.)
[Spain] [ohr-deh-nah-DOHR]

confused *confundido(a)*
[kohn-foon-DEE-doh (dah)]

cookie *galleta* (f.) [gah-YEH-tah]

to cost *costar* [kohs-TAHR]

country *país* (m.) [pahy-EES]

credit card *tarjeta* (f.) *de
crédito* [tahr-HEH-tah deh
KREH-dee-toh]

crib *cuna* (f.) [KOO-nah]

cup *taza* (f.), *copa* (f.) [TAH-sah, KOH-pah]

customs *aduana* (f.) [ah-DWAH-nah]

dark *oscuro(a)* [ohs-KOO-roh (rah)]

data *datos* (m. pl.) [DAH-tohs]

date *fecha* (f.) [FEH-chah]

daughter *hija* (f.) [EE-hah]

day *día* (m.) [DEE-yah]

debit card *tarjeta* (f.) de *débito* [tahr-HEH-tah deh DEH-bee-toh]

decaffeinated *descafeinado(a)* [dehs-kah-feh-yee-NAH-doh (dah)]

December *diciembre* [dee-see-YEHM-breh]

to decide *decidir* [deh-see-DEER]

to declare *declarar* [deh-klah-RAHR]

to deliver *entregar* [ehn-treh-GAHR]

dentist *dentista* (m./f.) [dehn-TEES-tah]

deodorant *desodorante* (m.) [deh-soh-doh-RAHN-teh]

department store *almacén* (m.) [ahl-mah-SEHN]

departure *salida* (f.) [sah-LEE-dah]

to describe *describir* [dehs-kree-BEER]

to desire *desear* [deh-seh-YAHR]

dessert *postre* (m.) [POHS-treh]

dictionary *diccionario* (m.) [deek-see-yoh-nah-REE-yoh]

difficult *difícil* [dee-FEE-seel]

dirty *sucio(a)* [SOO-see-yoh (yah)]

discount *descuento* (m.), *rebaja* (f.) [dehs-KWEHN-toh, rreh-BAH-hah]

to do *hacer* [ah-SEHR]

doctor *doctor(a)*, *médico(a)* [dohk-TOHR (dohk-TOH-rah), MEH-dee-koh (MEH-dee-kah)]

dog *perro* (m.) [PEH-rroh]

door *puerta* (f.) [PWEHR-tah]

downtown *centro* (m.) [SEHN-troh]

dozen *docena* (f.) [doh-SEH-nah]

dress *vestido* (m.) [behs-TEE-doh]

to drink *beber* [beh-BEHR]

during *durante* [doo-RAHN-teh]

each *cada* [KAH-dah]

ear *oreja* (f.) [oh-REH-hah]

early *temprano* [tehm-PRAH-noh]

to earn *ganar* [gah-NAHR]

east *este* (m.) [EHS-teh]

easy *fácil* [FAH-seel]

to eat *comer* [koh-MEHR]

egg *huevo* (m.) [HWEH-boh]

eight *ocho* [OH-choh]

eighteen *dieciocho* [dee-yehs-ee-OH-choh]

eighty *ochenta* [oh-CHEHN-tah]

electricity *electricidad* (f.) [eh-lehk-tree-see-DAHD]

elevator *ascensor* (m.) [ah-sehn-SOHR]

eleven *once* [OHN-seh]

email *correo* (m.) *electrónico* [koh-RREH-yoh eh-lehk-TROH-nee-koh]

employee *empleado(a)* [ehm-pleh-YAH-doh (dah)]

to end *terminar, concluir* [tehr-mee-NAHR, kohn-KLWEER]

English *inglés* [een-GLEHS]

to enjoy *gozar* [goh-SAHR]

enough *bastante, suficiente* [bahs-TAHN-teh, soo-fee-see-YEHN-teh]

entertainment guide *agenda* (f.) *cultural* [ah-HEHN-dah kool-too-RAHL]

entrance *entrada* (f.) [ehn-TRAH-dah]

evening *noche* (f.) [NOH-cheh]

exchange rate *tasa* (f.) *[tipo* (m.)*] de cambio* [TAH-sah (TEE-poh) deh KAHM-bee-yoh]

Excuse me. *Disculpe.* [dees-KOOL-peh]

exit *salida* (f.) [sah-LEE-dah]

to explain *explicar* [ehs-plee-KAHR]

eye *ojo* (m.) [OH-hoh]

facing *frente a* [FREHN-teh ah]

family *familia* (f.) [fah-MEEL-yah]

far (from) *lejos (de)* [LEH-hohs deh]

fare *tarifa* (f.) [tah-REE-fah]

father *padre* (m.) [PAH-dreh]

February *febrero* [feh-BREH-roh]

fifteen *quince* [KEEN-seh]

fifty *cincuenta* [seen-KWEHN-tah]

to find *encontrar* [ehn-kohn-TRAHR]

first *primer(o)(a)* [pree-MEHR (pree-MEH-roh) (pree-MEH-rah)]

fish *pescado* (m.) [pehs-KAH-doh]

fish store *pescadería* (f.) [pehs-kah-deh-REE-yah]

fitness center *gimnasio* (m.) [heem-NAH-see-yoh]

five *cinco* (m.) [SEEN-koh]

to fix *arreglar, reparar* [ah-RREH-glahr, rreh-pah-RAHR]

flight *vuelo* (m.) [BWEH-loh]

floor (story) *piso* (m.) [PEE-soh]

to follow *seguir* [seh-GEER]

food *comida* (f.) [koh-MEE-dah]

foot *pie* (m.) [pee-YEH]

for *para, por* [PAH-rah, pohr]

fork *tenedor* (m.) [teh-neh-DOHR]

forty *cuarenta* [kwah-REHN-tah]

four *cuatro* [KWAH-troh]

fourteen *catorce* [kah-TOHR-seh]

Friday *viernes* (m.) [bee-YEHR-nehs]

from *de, desde* [deh, DEHS-deh]

front, in front (of) *delante (de)* [deh-LAHN-teh (deh)]

gasoline *gasolina* (f.) [gah-soh-LEE-nah]

gate   *salida* (f.), *puerta* (f.)
[sah-LEE-dah, PWEHR-tah]

gift shop   *tienda* (f.) *de
regalos* [tee-YEHN-dah deh
rreh-GAH-lohs]

to give   *dar* [dahr]

glass   *vaso* (m.) [BAH-soh]

glove   *guante* (m.) [GWAHN-
teh]

to go   *ir* [eer]

to go out   *salir* [sah-LEER]

gold   *oro* (m.) [OH-roh]

good   *bueno(a)* [BWEH-noh
(nah)]

good-bye   *adiós* [ah-dee-
YOHS]

gray   *gris* [grees]

green   *verde* [BEHR-deh]

grocery store   *abacería*
(f.) [ah-bah-seh-REE-
yah], *almacén* (m.) [Latin
America] [ahl-mah-SEHN]

ground floor   *planta* (f.)
baja [PLAHN-tah BAH-hah]

guidebook   *guía* (f.) [GEE-
yah]

hair   *pelo* (m.) [PEH-loh], *el
cabello* (m.) [ehl kah-BEH-yoh]

half   *medio(a)* [MEH-dee-
yoh]

ham   *jamón* (m.) [hah-
MOHN]

hamburger   *hamburguesa*
(f.) [ahm-boor-GEH-sah]

hand   *mano* (f.) [MAH-noh]

handicap access   *acceso* (m.)
para los minusválidos [ahk-
SEH-soh PAH-rah lohs mee-
noos-BAH-lee-dohs]

handicap services   *servicios*
(m. pl.) *para los minusválidos*
[sehr-BEE-see-yohs PAH-rah
lohs mee-noos-BAH-lee-dohs]

handicapped *minusválido(a)*
[mee-noos-BAH-lee-doh
(dah)]

hanger   *percha* (f.) [PEHR-
chah]

happy   *alegre* [ah-LEH-greh]

hat   *sombrero* (m.) [sohm-
BREH-roh]

to have   *tener* [teh-NEHR]

to have to   *tener que +
infinitive* [teh-NEHR keh]

head   *cabeza* (f.) [kah-BEH-
sah]

to hear   *oír* [oy-EER]

heart   *corazón* (m.) [koh-rah-
SOHN]

hello   *hola* [OH-lah]

to help   *ayudar* [ah-yoo-
DAHR]

here   *aquí* [ah-KEE]

holiday   *fiesta* (f.) [fee-
YEHS-tah]

to hope   *esperar* [ehs-peh-
RAHR]

hospital   *hospital* (m.) [ohs-
pee-TAHL]

**hot, to be hot
(person)**   *tener calor* [teh-
NEHR kah-LOHR]

hot, to be hot (weather)
hacer calor [ah-SEHR kah-
LOHR]

hour   *hora* (f.) [OH-rah]

house   *casa* (f.) [KAH-sah]

housekeeping service
servicio (m.) *de limpieza* [sehr-
BEE-see-yoh deh leem-pee-
YEH-sah]

how   *¿cómo?* [KOH-moh]

how much, many
cuánto(s) [KWAHN-toh]

hundred *cien(to)* [see-YEHN-(toh)]

hungry (to be hungry) *tener hambre* [teh-NEHR AHM-breh]

hurry (to be in a hurry) *tener prisa* [teh-NEHR PREE-sah]

husband *esposo* (m.), *marido* (m.) [ehs-POH-soh, mah-REE-doh]

ice cream *helado* (m.) [eh-LAH-doh]

ice cubes *cubitos* (m. pl.) *de hielo* [koo-BEE-tohs deh ee-YEH-loh]

in *en* [ehn]

included *incluido(a)* [een-KLWEE-doh (dah)]

information *información* (f.) [een-fohr-mah-see-YOHN]

inside *adentro* [ah-DEHN-troh]

instead of *en lugar de, en vez de* [ehn loo-GAHR deh, ehn behs deh]

interpreter *interprete* (m./f.) [een-TEHR-preh-teh]

jacket *chaqueta* (f.), *saco* (m.) [chah-KEH-tah, SAH-koh]

January *enero* [eh-NEH-roh]

jar *frasco* (m.) [FRAHS-koh]

jelly *mermelada* (f.) [mehr-meh-LAH-dah]

jewelry store *joyería* (f.) [hoh-yeh-REE-yah]

juice *jugo* (m.) [Latin America], *zumo* (m.) [Spain] [HOO-goh, SOO-moh]

July *julio* [HOO-lee-yoh]

June *junio* [HOO-nee-yoh]

to keep *guardar* [GWAHR-dahr]

ketchup *salsa* (f.) *de tomate* [SAHL-sah deh toh-MAH-teh]

key *llave* (f.) [YAH-beh]

kitchen *cocina* (f.) [koh-SEE-nah]

knife *cuchillo* (m.) [koo-CHEE-yoh]

lamb *carne de cordero* (f.) [KAHR-neh deh kohr-DEH-roh]

lamp *lámpara* (f.) [LAHM-pah-rah]

to land *aterrizar* [ah-teh-rree-SAHR]

laptop (wireless) *portatíl (inalámbrico)* [pohr-tah-TEEL] [(ee-nah-LAHM-bree-koh)]

last *pasado(a), último(a)* [pah-SAH-doh (dah), OOL-tee-moh (mah)]

to last *durar* [doo-RAHR]

late *tarde* [TAHR-deh]

late in arriving *en retraso* [ehn rreh-TRAH-soh]

to learn *aprender* [ah-prehn-DEHR]

leather *cuero* (m.) [KWEH-roh]

to leave *dejar, salir* [deh-HAHR, sah-LEER]

left (direction) *izquierda* (f.) [ees-kee-YEHR-dah]

leg *pierna* (f.) [pee-YEHR-nah]

lemon *limón* (m.) [lee-MOHN]

to lend *prestar* [prehs-TAHR]

less *menos* [MEH-nohs]

letter *carta* (f.) [KAHR-tah]

lettuce *lechuga* (f.) [leh-CHOO-gah]

library *biblioteca* (f.) [bee-blee-yoh-TEH-kah]

light *claro(a)* [KLAH-roh (rah)]

to like *gustar* [goos-TAHR]

liquor store *tienda de licores* (f.) [tee-YEHN-dah deh lee-KOH-rehs]

to listen to *escuchar* [ehs-koo-CHAHR]

little *poco(a)* [POH-koh (kah)]

to live *vivir* [bee-BEER]

long *largo(a)* [LAHR-goh (gah)]

to look at *mirar* [mee-RAHR]

to look for *buscar* [boos-KAHR]

to lose *perder* [pehr-DEHR]

lucky (to be lucky) *tener suerte* [teh-NEHR SWEHR-teh]

magazine *revista* (f.) [rreh-BEES-tah]

mailbox *buzón* (m.) [boo-SOHN]

to make *hacer* [ah-SEHR]

makeup *maquillaje* (m.) [mah-kee-YAH-heh]

mall *centro* (m.) *comercial* [SEHN-troh koh-mehr-see-YAHL]

manager *director(a)* [dee-rehk-TOHR] [(dee-rehk-TOH-rah)]

map *mapa* (m.) [MAH-pah]

March *marzo* [MAHR-soh]

market *mercado* (m.) [mehr-KAH-doh]

married *casado(a)* [kah-SAH-doh (dah)]

match *fósforo* (m.) [FOHS-foh-roh]

May *mayo* [MAH-yoh]

mayonnaise *mayonesa* (f.) [mah-yoh-NEH-sah]

to mean *significar* [seeg-nee-fee-KAHR]

meat *carne* (f.) [KAHR-neh]

medicine *medicamento* (m.), *medicina* (f.) [meh-dee-kah-MEHN-toh, meh-dee-SEE-nah]

menu *carta* (f.), *menú* (m.) [KAHR-tah, meh-NOO]

message *mensaje* (m.) [mehn-SAH-heh]

midnight *medianoche* (f.) [meh-dee-yah-NOH-cheh]

milk *leche* (f.) [LEH-cheh]

mineral water *agua* (f.) *mineral* [AH-gwah mee-neh-RAHL]

minute *minuto* (m.) [mee-NOO-toh]

mirror *espejo* (m.) [ehs-PEH-hoh]

Monday *lunes* (m.) [LOO-nehs]

money *dinero* (m.) [dee-NEH-roh]

money exchange *casa* (f.) *de cambio* [KAH-sah deh KAHM-bee-yoh]

month *mes* (m.) [mehs]

monument *monumento* (m.) [moh-noo-MEHN-toh]

more *más* [mahs]

morning *mañana* (f.) [mah-NYAH-nah]

mother *madre* (f.) [MAH-dreh]

mouth *boca* (f.) [BOH-kah]

mouthwash *enjuague* (m.) *bucal* [ehn-HWAH-geh boo-KAHL]

movie *película* (f.) [peh-LEE-koo-lah]

movies *cine* (m.) [SEE-neh]

museum *museo* (m.) [moo-SEH-yoh]

mushroom *champiñon* (m.) [cham-pee-NYOHN]

mustard *mostaza* (f.) [mohs-TAH-sah]

napkin *servilleta* (f.) [sehr-bee-YEH-tah]

narrow *estrecho(a)* [ehs-TREH-choh (chah)]

near *cerca (de)* [SEHR-kah (deh)]

necessary *necesario(a)* [neh-seh-SAH-ree-yoh (yah)]

to need *necesitar* [neh-seh-see-TAHR]

new *nuevo(a)* [NWEH-boh (bah)]

news *noticias* (f. pl.) [noh-TEE-see-yahs]

newspaper *periódico* (m.) [peh-ree-YOH-dee-koh]

newsstand *quiosco* (m.) *de periódicos* [kee-YOHS-koh deh] [peh-ree-YOH-dee-kohs]

next *próximo* [PROHK-see-moh]

next to *al lado de* [ah LAH-doh deh]

nice *simpático(a), amable* [seem-PAH-tee-koh (kah), ah-MAH-bleh]

nine *nueve* [NWEH-beh]

nineteen *diecinueve* [dee-yehs-ee-NWEH-beh]

ninety *noventa* [noh-BEHN-tah]

nobody *nadie* [NAH-dee-yeh]

noon *mediodía* (m.) [meh-dee-yoh-DEE-yah]

north *norte* (m.) [NOHR-teh]

November *noviembre* [noh-bee-YEHM-breh]

now *ahora* [ah-OH-rah]

number *número* (m.) [NOO-meh-roh]

ocean *mar* (m.) [mahr]

October *octubre* [ohk-TOO-breh]

of *de* [deh]

of course *por supuesto, claro* [pohr soo-PWEHS-toh, KLAH-roh]

office *oficina* (f.) [oh-fee-SEE-nah]

office (medical) *consultorio* (m.) [kohn-sool-TOH-ree-yoh]

often *a menudo* [ah meh-NOO-doh]

old *viejo(a)* [BEE-yeh-hoh (hah)]

on *en* [ehn]

one *un, uno, una* [oon, OO-noh, OO-nah]

onion *cebolla* (f.) [seh-BOH-yah]

to open *abrir* [ah-BREER]

opposite *frente a* [FREHN-teh ah]

orange (color) *anaranjado(a)* [ah-nah-rahn-HAH-doh (dah)]

orange (fruit) *naranja* [nah-RAHN-hah]

to order *mandar* [mahn-DAHR]

outside *afuera* [ah-FWEH-rah]

package *paquete* (m.) [pah-KEH-teh]

pain *dolor* (m.) [doh-LOHR]

pants *pantalones* (m. pl.) [pahn-tah-LOH-nehs]

paper *papel* (m.) [pah-PEHL]

parents *padres* (m. pl.) [PAH-drehs]

park *parque* (m.) [PAHR-keh]

to participate *participar* [pahr-tee-see-PAHR]

passport *pasaporte* (m.) [pah-sah-POHR-teh]

password *contraseña* (f.) [kohn-trah-SEH-nyah]

to pay *pagar* [pah-GAHR]

pencil *lápiz* (m.) [LAH-pees]

pepper *pimienta* (f.) [pee-mee-YEHN-tah]

pharmacy *farmacia* (f.) [fahr-MAH-see-yah]

to phone *telefonear* [teh-leh-foh-neh-YAHR]

phone book *guía* (f.) *telefónica* [GEE-yah teh-leh-FOH-nee-kah]

phone card *tarjeta* (f.) *telefónica* [tahr-HEH-tah teh-leh-FOH-nee-kah]

photocopy *fotocopia* [foh-toh-KOH-pee-yah]

phone number *número* (m.) *de teléfono* [NOO-meh-roh deh teh-LEH-foh-noh]

pill *pastilla* (f.) [pahs-TEE-yah]

pillow *almohada* (f.) [ahl-moh-AH-dah]

pink *rosado(a)* [RROH-sah-doh (dah)]

place *lugar* (m.) [loo-GAHR]

plane *avión* (m.) [ah-bee-YOHN]

plate *plato* (m.) [PLAH-toh]

to play games, sports *jugar* [hoo-GAHR]

please *por favor* [pohr fah-BOHR]

pocketbook *bolsa* (f.) [BOHL-sah]

police officer *agente* (m./f.) *de policía* [ah-HEHN-teh deh poh-lee-SEE-yah]

police station *comisaría* (f.) *de policía* [koh-mee-sah-REE-yah deh poh-lee-SEE_yah]

pool *piscina* (f.) [pee-SEE-nah]

poor *pobre* [POH-breh]

postage *franqueo* (m.) [frahn-KEH-yoh]

postcard *postal* (m.) [pohs-TAHL]

potato *papa* (f.), *patata* (f.) [PAH-pah, pah-TAH-tah]

to prefer *preferir* [preh-feh-REER]

prescription *receta* (f.) [rreh-SEH-tah]

pretty *bonito(a)* [boh-NEE-toh (tah)]

price *precio* (m.) [PREH-see-yoh]

problem *problema* (m.) [proh-BLEH-mah]

to purchase *comprar* [kohm-PRAHR]

purple *morado(a)* [moh-RAH-doh (dah)]

to put *poner* [poh-NEHR]

quarter   *cuarto* (m.) [KWAHR-toh]

question   *pregunta* (f.) [preh-GOON-tah]

quickly   *rápidamente* [RRAH-pee-dah-mehn-teh]

to read   *leer* [leh-YEHR]

receipt   *recibo* (m.) [rreh-SEE-boh]

to receive   *recibir* [rreh-see-BEER]

to recommend   *recomendar* [rreh-koh-mehn-DAHR]

red   *rojo(a)* [RROH-hoh (hah)]

refund   *reembolso* [rreh-yehm-BOHL-soh]

to remember *recordar* [rreh-kohr-DAHR]

to rent   *alquilar* [ahl-kee-LAHR]

to repair   *reparar* [rreh-pah-RAHR]

restaurant   *restaurante* (m.) [rrehs-tow-RAHN-teh]

retired   *jubilado(a)* [hoo-bee-LAH-doh (dah)]

to return   *regresar; volver* [rreh-greh-SAHR, bohl-BEHR]

to return (item) *devolver* [deh-bohl-BEHR]

rice   *arroz* (m.) [ah-RROHS]

rideshare   *vehículo* (m.) *compartido* [beh-EE-koo-loh kohm-pahr-TEE-doh]

right (direction)   *derecha* (f.) [deh-REH-chah]

room   *cuarto* (m.), *habitación* (f.) [KWAHR-toh, ah-bee-tah-see-YOHN]

safe   *caja* (f.) *fuerte* [KAH-hah FWEHR-teh]

salad   *ensalada* (f.) [ehn-sah-LAH-dah]

sale (bargain)   *venta* (f.), *(ganga* [f.]) [BEHN-tah, (GAHN-gah)]

salesperson   *vendedor(a)* [behn-deh-DOHR] [(behn-deh-DOH-rah)]

salt   *sal* (f.) [sahl]

sample   *muestra* (f.) [MWEHS-trah]

Saturday   *sábado* (m.) [SAH-bah-doh]

sauce   *salsa* (f.) [SAHL-sah]

saucer   *platillo* (m.) [plah-TEE-yoh]

to say   *decir* [deh-SEER]

scissors   *tijeras* (f. pl.) [tee-HEH-rahs]

seafood   *mariscos* (m. pl.) [mah-REES-kohs]

seat   *asiento* (m.) [ah-see-YEHN-toh]

seatbelt   *cinturón* (m.) *de seguridad* [seen-too-ROHN deh seh-goo-ree-DAHD]

to see   *ver* [behr]

to sell   *vender* [behn-DEHR]

to send   *mandar; enviar* [mahn-DAHR, ehn-bee-YAHR]

September   *septiembre* [sehp-tee-YEHM-breh]

seven   *siete* [see-YEH-teh]

seventeen   *diecisiete* [dee-yehs-ee-see-YEH-teh]

seventy   *setenta* [seh-TEHN-tah]

shampoo   *champú* (m.) [chahm-POO]

shirt   *camisa* (f.) [kah-MEE-sah]

shoe *zapato* (m.) [sah-PAH-toh]

shoe store *zapatería* (f.) [sah-pah-teh-REE-yah]

short *bajo(a), corto(a)* (f.) [BAH-hoh (hah), KOHR-toh (tah)]

show *espectáculo* (m.) [ehs-pehk-TAH-koo-loh]

to show *enseñar, mostrar* [ehn-seh-NYAHR, mohs-TRAHR]

sick *enfermo(a)* [ehn-FEHR-moh (mah)]

to sign *firmar* [feer-MAHR]

silk *seda* (f.) [SEH-dah]

silver *plata* (f.) [PLAH-tah]

since *desde* [DEHS-deh]

single (unmarried) *soltero(a)* [sohl-TEH-roh (rah)]

sister *hermana* (f.) [ehr-MAH-nah]

six *seis* [SEHY-ees]

sixteen *dieciséis* [dee-yehs-ee-SEHY-ees]

sixty *sesenta* [seh-SEHN-tah]

skirt *falda* (f.) [FAHL-dah]

slowly *lentamente* [lehn-tah-MEHN-teh]

small *pequeño(a)* [peh-KEH-nyoh (nyah)]

to smoke *fumar* [foo-MAHR]

sneakers *zapatillas* (f. pl.) [Spain] sah-pah-TEE-yahs, *tenis* (m. pl.) [Spanish America] [TEH-nees]

sock *calcetín* (m.) [kahl-seh-TEEN], *media* (f.) [Latin America] MEH-dee-yah

soda *gaseosa* (f.), *refresco* (m.), *soda* (f.) [gah-seh-YOH-sah, rreh-FREHS-koh, SOH-dah]

son *hijo* (m.) [EE-hoh]

soon *pronto* [PROHN-toh]

soup *sopa* (f.) [SOH-pah]

south *sur* (m.) [soor]

souvenir shop *tienda* (f.) *de recuerdos* [tee-YEHN-dah deh rreh-KWEHR-dohs]

Spanish *español* (m.) [ehs-pah-NYOHL]

to speak *hablar* [ah-BLAHR]

to spend money *gastar* [gahs-TAHR]

to spend time *pasar* [pah-SAHR]

spicy *picante* [pee-KAHN-teh]

spoon *cuchara* (f.) [koo-CHAH-rah]

spring *primavera* (f.) [pree-mah-BEH-rah]

stadium *estadio* (m.) [ehs-TAH-dee-yoh]

stamp *sello* (m.) [SEH-yoh]

still *todavía* [toh-dah-BEE-yah]

stomach *estómago* (m.) [ehs-TOH-mah-goh]

stone *piedra* (f.) [pee-YEH-drah]

stopover *escala* (f.) [ehs-KAH-lah]

store *tienda* (f.) [tee-YEHN-dah]

strawberry *fresa* (f.) [FREH-sah], *frutilla* (f.) [Latin America] [froo-TEE-yah]

street *calle* (f.) [KAH-yeh]

subway *metro* (m.) [MEH-troh], *subterráneo* (m.) [Latin America] [ehl soob-teh-RRAH-neh-yoh]

subway station *estación* (f.) *de metro* [ehs-tah-see-YOHN deh MEH-troh]

sugar *azúcar* (m.) [ah-SOO-kahr]

suitcase *maleta* (f.) [mah-LEH-tah]

summer *verano* (m.) [beh-RAH-noh]

Sunday *domingo* (m.) [doh-MEEN-goh]

sunglasses *gafas* (f. pl.) *de sol* [GAH-fahs deh sohl]

supermarket *supermercado* (m.) [soo-pehr-mehr-KAH-doh]

sweater *suéter* (m.) [SWEH-tehr]

sweet *dulce* [DOOL-seh]

table *mesa* (f.) [MEH-sah]

to take *tomar* [toh-MAHR]

to take place *tener lugar* [teh-NEHR loo-GAHR]

to talk *hablar* [ah-BLAHR]

tall *alto(a)* [AHL-toh (tah)]

tax *impuesto* (m.) [eem-PWEHS-toh]

taxi *taxi* (m.) [TAHK-see]

taxi stand *parada* (f.) *de taxi* [pah-RAH-dah deh TAHK-see]

tea *té* (m.) [teh]

teaspoon *cucharita* (f.) [koo-chah-REE-tah]

T-shirt *camiseta* (f.), *playera* (f.) [kah-mee-SEH-tah, plah-YEH-rah]

telephone *teléfono* (m.) [teh-LEH-foh-noh]

to telephone *telefonear* [teh-leh-foh-neh-YAHR]

television *televisión* (f.) [teh-leh-bee-see-YOHN]

to tell *decir* [deh-SEER]

ten *diez* [dee-YEHS]

thank you *muchas gracias* [MOO-chahs GRAH-see-yahs]

theater *teatro* (m.) [teh-YAH-troh]

then *después, luego* [dehs-PWEHS, LWEH-goh]

thirteen *trece* [TREH-seh]

thirty *treinta* [TREHYN-tah]

thousand *mil* [meel]

three *tres* [trehs]

throat *garganta* (f.) [gahr-GAHN-tah]

through *por* [pohr]

Thursday *jueves* (m.) [HWEH-behs]

ticket *billete* (m.) [bee-YEH-teh]

time *tiempo* (m.), *hora* (f.) [tee-YEHM-poh, OH-rah]

time (on time) *a tiempo* [ah tee-YEHM-poh]

tip (gratuity) *propina* (f.) [proh-PEE-nah]

tissue *pañuelo* (m.) *de papel* [pah-nyoo-WEH-loh deh pah-PEHL]

to *a* [ah]

tobacco store *tabaquería* (f.) [tah-bah-keh-REE-yah]

today *hoy* [ohy]

tomato *tomate* (m.) [toh-MAH-teh]

tomorrow *mañana* [mah-NYAH-nah]

too (also) *también* [tahm-bee-YEHN]

too much *demasiado* [deh-mah-see-YAH-doh]

tooth *diente* (m.) [dee-YEHN-teh]

toothbrush *cepillo* (m.) *de dientes* [seh-PEE-yoh deh dee-YEHN-tehs]

toothpaste *pasta* (f.) *dentífrica* [PAHS-tah dehn-tee-FREE-kah]

towel *toalla* (f.) [toh-WAH-yah]

train *tren* (m.) [trehn]

train station *estación de tren* [ehs-tah-see-YOHN deh trehn]

to travel *viajar* (f.) [bee-yah-HAHR]

trip *viaje* (m.) [bee-YAH-heh]

Tuesday *martes* (m.) [MAHR-tehs]

turkey *pavo* (m.) [PAH-boh]

twelve *doce* [DOH-seh]

twenty *veinte* [BEHYN-teh]

two *dos* [dohs]

umbrella *paraguas* (m.) [pah-RAH-gwahs]

under *debajo de* [deh-BAH-hoh deh]

to understand *comprender, entender* [kohm-prehn-DEHR, ehn-tehn-DEHR]

United States *Estados Unidos* (m. pl.) [ehs-TAH-dohs oo-NEE-dohs]

until *hasta* [AHS-tah]

upon *sobre* [SOH-breh]

to use *usar* [OO-sahr]

vegan *vegano(a)* [beh-GAH-noh (nah)]

vegetable *verdura* (f.) [behr-DOO-rah]

vegetarian *vegetariano(a)* [beh-heh-tah-ree-YAH-noh (nah)]

very *muy* [mwee]

to visit *visitar* [bee-see-TAHR]

to wait for *esperar* [ehs-peh-RAHR]

wallet *cartera* (f.) [kahr-TEH-rah]

to want *querer* [keh-REHR]

watch *reloj* (m.) [rreh-LOH]

water *agua* (f.) [AH-gwah]

weather *tiempo* (m.) [tee-YEHM-poh], *clima* (m.) [Latin America] [ehl KLEE-mah]

weather forecast *pronóstico* (m.) [proh-NOHS-tee-koh]

Wednesday *miércoles* (m.) [mee-YEHR-koh-lehs]

week *semana* (f.) [seh-MAH-nah]

welcome (you're welcome) *de nada* [deh NAH-dah]

well *bien* [bee-YEHN]

west *oeste* (m.) [oh-WEHS-teh]

what *¿qué?* [keh]

when *¿cuándo?* [KWAHN-doh]

where *¿dónde?* [DOHN-deh]

which *¿cuál(es)?* [kwahl (KWAH-lehs)]

white *blanco(a)* [BLAHN-koh (kah)]

who(m) *¿quién(es)?* [kee-YEHN (kee-YEH-nehs)]

why *¿por qué?* [pohr keh]

wide *ancho(a)* [AHN-choh (chah)]

widow(er) *viuda*
(viudo) [bee-YOO-dah (doh)]

wife *esposa* (f.) [ehs-POH-sah]

window (car) *ventana* (f.)
(ventanilla) [f.] [behn-TAH-nah] [(behn-tah-NEE-yah)]

wine *vino* (m.) [BEE-noh]

winter *invierno* (m.) [een-bee-YEHR-noh]

without *sin* [seen]

wool *lana* (f.) [LAH-nah]

work *trabajar* [trah-bah-HAHR]

work (function)
funcionar [foon-see-yoh-NAHR]

to write *escribir* [ehs-kree-BEER]

yellow *amarillo(a)* [ah-mah-REE-yoh (yah)]

yesterday *ayer* [ah-YEHR]

young *joven* [HOH-behn]

Spanish to English Dictionary

a [ah] at, to

a menudo [ah meh-NOO-doh] often

a tiempo [ah tee-YEHM-poh] time (on time)

abacería (f.) [ah-bah-seh-REE-yah] grocery store

abordar [ah-bohr-DAHR] to board

abril [AH-breel] April

abrir [ah-BREER] to open

acompañar [ah-kohm-pah-NYAHR] to accompany

adentro [ah-DEHN-troh] inside

adiós [ah-dee-YOHS] good-bye

aduana (f.) [ah-DWAH-nah] customs

aerolínea (f.) [ahy-roh-LEE-neh-yah] airline

aeropuerto (m.) [ahy-roh-PWEHR-toh] airport

afuera [ah-FWEH-rah] outside

agosto [ah-GOHS-toh] August

agua (f.) [AH-gwah] water

ahora [ah-OH-rah] now

al lado de [ah LAH-doh deh] next to

alegre [ah-LEH-greh] happy

almacén (m.) [ahl-mah-SEHN] department store, grocery store [Latin America]

almohada (f.) [ahl-moh-AH-dah] pillow

alquilar [ahl-kee-LAHR] to rent

alrededor (de) [ahl-reh-deh-DOHR (deh)] around

alto(a) [AHL-toh (tah)] tall

amarillo(a) [ah-mah-REE-yoh (yah)] yellow

anaranjado(a) [ah-nah-rahn-HAH-doh (dah)] orange (color)

ancho(a) [AHN-choh (chah)] wide

antes (de) [AHN-tehs (deh)] before

aprender [ah-prehn-DEHR] to learn

aquí [ah-KEE] here

arreglar [ah-RREH-glahr] to adjust

arroz (m.) [ah-RROHS] rice

ascensor (m.) [ah-sehn-SOHR] elevator

asiento (m.) [ah-see-YEHN-toh] seat

aterrizar [ah-teh-rree-SAHR] to land

avión (m.) [ah-bee-YOHN] plane

ayer [ah-YEHR] yesterday

ayudar [ah-yoo-DAHR] to help

azúcar (m.) [ah-SOO-kahr] sugar

azul [ah-SOOL] blue

bajo(a) [BAH-hoh (hah)] short

banco (m.) [BAHN-koh] bank

baño(s) (m. pl.) [BAH-nyoh(s)] bathroom

barco (m.) [BAHR-koh] boat

bastante [bahs-TAHN-teh] enough

beber [beh-BEHR] to drink

biblioteca (f.) [bee-blee-yoh-TEH-kah] library

bien [bee-YEHN] well

billete (m.) [bee-YEH-teh] bill (money), ticket

blanco(a) [BLAHN-koh (kah)] white

blusa (f.) [BLOO-sah] blouse

boca (f.) [BOH-kah] mouth

boleto (m.) [boh-LEH-toh] ticket

bolígrafo (m.) [boh-LEE-grah-foh] ballpoint pen

bolsa (f.) [BOHL-sah] bag, pocketbook

bonito(a) [boh-NEE-toh (tah)] pretty

botas (f. pl.) [BOH-tahs] boots

botella (f.) [boh-TEH-yah] bottle

botones (m.) [boh-TOH-nehs] bellman

brazo (m.) [BRAH-soh] arm

bueno(a) [BWEH-noh (nah)] good

buscar [boos-KAHR] to look for

buzón (m.) [boo-SOHN] mailbox

cabeza (f.) [kah-BEH-sah] head

cada [KAH-dah] each

café (m.) [kah-FEH] coffee

caja (f.) *(fuerte)* [KAH-hah (FWEHR-teh)] box (safe)

cajero(a) *(automático)* [kah-HEH-roh (rah)] [(ow-toh-MAH-tee-koh)] cashier (ATM)

calcetín (m.) [kahl-seh-TEEN] sock

calculadora (f.) [kahl-koo-lah-DOH-rah] calculator

calle (f.) [KAH-yeh] street

cambiar [kahm-bee-YAHR] to change

camisa (f.) [kah-MEE-sah] shirt

camiseta (f.), *playera* (f.) [kah-mee-SEH-tah, plah-YEH-rah] tee shirt

carne (f.) [KAHR-neh] meat

carne (f.) *de vaca* [KAHR-neh deh BAH-kah] beef

carne (f.) *de cordero* [KAHR-neh deh kohr-DEH-roh] lamb

carnicería (f.) [kahr-nee-seh-REE-yah] butcher shop

carta (f.) [KAHR-tah] letter

carta (f.), *menú* (m.) [KAHR-tah, meh-NOO] menu

cartera (f.) [kahr-TEH-rah] wallet

casa (f.) [KAH-sah] house

casa (f.) *de cambio* [KAH-sah deh KAHM-bee-yoh] money exchange

casado(a) [kah-SAH-doh (dah)] married

casi [KAH-see] almost

catorce [kah-TOHR-seh] fourteen

cebolla (f.) [seh-BOH-yah] onion

cenicero (m.) [seh-nee-SEH-roh] ashtray

centro (m.) [SEHN-troh] downtown

centro (m.) *comercial* [SEHN-troh koh-mehr-see-YAHL] mall

cepillo (m.) *de dientes* [seh-PEE-yoh deh dee-YEHN-tehs] toothbrush

cerca (de) [SEHR-kah (deh)] near

cereza (f.) [seh-REH-sah] cherry

cerrar [seh-RAHR] to close

cerveza (f.) [sehr-BEH-sah] beer

champiñon (m.) [cham-pee-NYOHN] mushroom

champú (m.) [chahm-POO] shampoo

chaqueta (f.) [chah-KEH-tah] jacket

cheque (m.) [CHEH-keh] check

cien (to) [see-YEHN (toh)] hundred

cinco (m.) [SEEN-koh] five

cincuenta [seen-KWEHN-tah] fifty

cine (m.) [SEE-neh] movies

cinturón (m.) *de seguridad* [seen-too-ROHN deh seh-goo-ree-DAHD] seatbelt

cita (f.) [SEE-tah] appointment

claro(a) [KLAH-roh (rah)] light

cobrar un cheque [koh-BRAHR oon CHEH-keh] to cash a check

coche (m.) [KOH-cheh] car

cocina (f.) [koh-SEE-nah] kitchen

comenzar [koh-mehn-SAHR] to begin

comer [koh-MEHR] to eat

comida (f.) [koh-MEE-dah]
food

comisaría (f.) *de policía*
[koh-mee-sah-REE-yah deh
poh-lee-SEE-yah] police
station

¿cómo? [KOH-moh] how

comprar [kohm-PRAHR] to
buy

comprender [kohm-prehn-
DEHR] to understand

computadora (f.) [kohm-poo-
tah-DOH-rah] computer

concluir [kohn-KLWEER] to
conclude

confundido(a) [kohn-foon-
DEE-doh (dah)] confused

consulado (m.) *americano*
[kohn-soo-LAH-doh ah-meh-
ree-KAH-noh] American
consulate

consultorio (m.) [kohn-
sool-TOH-ree-yoh] office
(medical)

contra [KOHN-trah] against

contraseña (f.) [kohn-trah-
SEH-nyah] password

copa (f.) [KOH-pah] glass

corazón (m.) [koh-rah-SOHN]
heart

correo (m.) *electrónico* [koh-
RREH-yoh eh-lehk-TROH-nee-
koh] email

corto(a) [KOHR-toh (tah)]
short

costar [kohs-TAHR] to cost

cuadra (f.) [KWAH-drah]
block (street)

¿cuál(es)? [kwahl (KWAH-
lehs)] which

¿cuándo? [KWAHN-doh]
when

¿cuánto(s) [KWAHN-toh(s)]
how much, many

cuarenta [kwah-REHN-tah]
forty

cuarto (m.) [KWAHR-toh]
quarter, room

cuatro [KWAH-troh] four

cubitos (m. pl.) *de hielo* [koo-
BEE-tohs deh ee-YEH-loh]
ice cubes

cuchara (f.) [koo-CHAH-rah]
spoon

cucharita (f.) [koo-chah-REE-
tah] teaspoon

cuchillo (m.) [koo-CHEE-yoh]
knife

cuenta (f.) [KWEHN-tah] bill
(restaurant)

cuero (m.) [KWEH-roh]
leather

cuna (f.) [KOO-nah] crib

curita (f.) [koo-REE-tah]
Band-Aid

dar [dahr] to give

datos (m. pl.) [DAH-tohs]
data

de [deh] of, from, about

de nada [deh NAH-dah]
you're welcome

de nuevo [deh NWEH-boh]
again

debajo de [deh-BAH-hoh deh]
below, beneath, under

decidir [deh-see-DEER] to
decide

decir [deh-SEER] to say,
to tell

declarar [deh-klah-RAHR] to declare

dejar [deh-HAHR] to leave

delante (de) [deh-LAHN-teh (deh)] front, in front (of)

demasiado [deh-mah-see-YAH-doh] too much

derecha (f.) [deh-REH-chah] right (direction)

describir [dehs-kree-BEER] to describe

descuento (m.) [dehs-KWEHN-toh] discount

desde [DEHS-deh] since, from

desear [deh-seh-YAHR] to desire

después [desh-PWEHS] then, after

después (de) [dehs-PWEHS (deh)] after

detrás (de) [deh-TRAHS (deh)] behind

devolver [deh-bohl-BEHR] to return (item)

día (m.) [DEE-yah] day

diccionario (m.) [deek-see-yoh-NAH-ree-yoh] dictionary

diciembre [dee-see-YEHM-breh] December

diecinueve [dee-yehs-ee-NWEH-beh] nineteen

dieciocho [dee-yehs-ee-OH-choh] eighteen

dieciséis [dee-yehs-ee-SEHY-ees] sixteen

diecisiete [dee-yehs-ee-see-YEH-teh] seventeen

diente (m.) [dee-YEHN-teh] tooth

diez [dee-YEHS] ten

difícil [dee-FEE-seel] difficult

dinero (m.) [dee-NEH-roh] cash, money

dirección (f.) [dee-rehk-see-YOHN] address

Disculpe. [dees-KOOL-peh] Excuse me.

disponible [dees-poh-NEE-bleh] available

doce [DOH-seh] twelve

docena (f.) [doh-SEH-nah] dozen

dolor (m.) [doh-LOHR] pain

domingo (m.) [doh-MEEN-goh] Sunday

¿dónde? [DOHN-deh] where

dos [dohs] two

dulce, dulces (m. pl.) [DOOL-seh(s)] sweet, sweets

dulcería (f.) [dool-seh-REE-yah] candy store

durante [doo-RAHN-teh] during

durar [doo-RAHR] to last

embajada (f.) *americana* [ehm-bah-HAH-dah ah-meh-ree-KAH-nah] American embassy

empezar [ehm-peh-SAHR] to begin

empleado(a) [ehm-pleh-YAH-doh (dah)] employee

en [ehn] in, on

en lugar de [ehn loo-GAHR deh] instead of

en retraso [ehn rreh-TRAH-soh] late in arriving

en vez de [ehn behs deh] instead of

encima de [ehn-SEE-mah deh] above, on top of

encontrar [ehn-kohn-TRAHR] to find

enero [eh-NEH-roh] January

enfermo(a) [ehn-FEHR-moh (mah)] sick

enjuague (m.) *bucal* [ehn-HWAH-geh boo-KAHL] mouthwash

ensalada (f.) [ehn-sah-LAH-dah] salad

enseñar [ehn-seh-NYAHR] to show

entender [ehn-tehn-DEHR] to understand

entrada (f.) [ehn-TRAH-dah] entrance

entre [EHN-treh] among, between

entregar [ehn-treh-GAHR] to deliver

enviar [ehn-bee-YAHR] to send

escala (f.) [ehs-KAH-lah] stopover

escribir [ehs-kree-BEER] to write

escuchar [ehs-koo-CHAHR] to listen (to)

español (m.) [ehs-pah-NYOHL] [Spanish]

espectáculo (m.) [ehs-pehk-TAH-koo-loh] show

espejo (m.) [ehs-PEH-hoh] mirror

esperar [ehs-peh-RAHR] to hope, to wait for

esposa (f.) [ehs-POH-sah] wife

esposo (m.) [ehs-POH-soh] husband

estación (f.) *de metro* [ehs-tah-see-YOHN deh MEH-troh] subway station

estación (f.) *de tren* [ehs-tah-see-YOHN deh trehn] train station

estadio (m.) [ehs-TAH-dee-yoh] stadium

Estados Unidos (m. pl.) [ehs-TAH-dohs oo-NEE-dohs] United States

estar [ehs-TAHR] to be

este (m.) [EHS-teh] east

estómago (m.) [ehs-TOH-mah-goh] stomach

estrecho(a) [ehs-TREH-choh (chah)] narrow

explicar [ehs-plee-KAHR] to explain

fácil [FAH-seel] easy

factura (f.) [fahk-TOO-rah] bill (commerce)

falda (f.) [FAHL-dah] skirt

farmacia (f.) [fahr-MAH-see-yah] pharmacy

febrero [feh-BREH-roh] February

fecha (f.) [FEH-chah] date

fiesta (f.) [fee-YEHS-tah] holiday

firmar [feer-MAHR] to sign

fósforo (m.) [FOHS-foh-roh] match

franqueo (m.) [frahn-KEH-yoh] postage

frasco (m.) [FRAHS-koh] jar

frente a [FREHN-teh ah] facing, opposite

fresa (f.) [FREH-sah] strawberry

fumar [foo-MAHR] to smoke

funcionar [foon-see-yoh-NAHR] work (function)

gafas de sol (f. pl.) [GAH-fahs deh sohl] sunglasses

galleta (f.) [gah-YEH-tah] cookie

ganar [gah-NAHR] to earn

ganga (f.) [GAHN-gah] sale, bargain

garganta (f.) [gahr-GAHN-tah] throat

gaseosa (f.) [gah-seh-YOH-sah] soda

gastar [gahs-TAHR] to spend money

gato (m.) [GAH-toh] cat

gozar [goh-SAHR] to enjoy

gris [grees] gray

guante (m.) [GWAHN-teh] glove

guardar [GWAHR-dahr] to keep

guía (f.) [GEE-yah] guidebook

guía (f.) *telefónica* [GEE-yah teh-leh-FOH-nee-kah] telephone book

gustar [goos-TAHR] to like

habitación (f.) [ah-bee-tah-see-YOHN] room

hablar [ah-BLAHR] to speak, to talk

hace + period of time [AH-seh] ago

hacer [ah-SEHR] to do, to make

hacer calor [ah-SEHR kah-LOHR] hot, to be hot (weather)

hacer frío [ah-SEHR FREE-yoh] cold, to be cold (weather)

hasta [AHS-tah] until

helado (m.) [eh-LAH-doh] ice cream

hermana (f.) [ehr-MAH-nah] sister

hermano (m.) [ehr-MAH-noh] brother

hija (f.) [EE-hah] daughter

hijo (m.) [EE-hoh] son

hola [OH-lah] hello

hora (f.) [OH-rah] hour, time

hoy [ohy] today

huevo (m.) [HWEH-boh] egg

iglesia (f.) [ee-GLEH-see-yah] church

impuesto (m.) [eem-PWEHS-toh] tax

incluido(a) [een-KLWEE-doh (dah)] included

inglés [een-GLEHS] English

invierno (m.) [een-bee-YEHR-noh] winter

ir [eer] to go

izquierda (f.) [ees-kee-YEHR-dah] left (direction)

jamón (m.) [hah-MOHN] ham

joven [HOH-behn] young

joyería (f.) [hoh-yeh-REE-yah] jewelry store

jubilado(a) [hoo-bee-LAH-doh (dah)] retired

jueves (m.) [HWEH-behs]
Thursday

jugar [hoo-GAHR] to play
games, sports

jugo (m.) [HOO-goh] juice

julio [HOO-lee-yoh] July

junio [HOO-nee-yoh] June

lámpara (f.) [LAHM-pah-rah]
lamp

lana (f.) [LAH-nah] wool

lápiz (m.) [LAH-pees] pencil

largo(a) [LAHR-goh (gah)]
long

lata (f.) [LAH-tah] can

leche (f.) [LEH-cheh] milk

lechuga (f.) [leh-CHOO-gah]
lettuce

leer [leh-YEHR] to read

lejos (de) [LEH-hohs (deh)]
far (from)

lentamente [lehn-tah-MEHN-
teh] slowly

librería (f.) [lee-breh-REE-
yah] bookstore

libro (m.) [LEE-broh] book

limón (m.) [lee-MOHN]
lemon

limpio(a) [LEEM-pee-yoh
(yah)] clean

llamar [yah-MAHR] to call

llave (f.) [YAH-beh] key

llegar [yeh-GAHR] to arrive

lugar (m.) [loo-GAHR] place

lunes (m.) [LOO-nehs]
Monday

madre (f.) [MAH-dreh]
mother

maleta (f.) [mah-LEH-tah]
suitcase

malo(a) [MAH-loh (lah)] bad

mañana [mah-NYAH-nah]
tomorrow, morning (f.)

mandar [mahn-DAHR] to
order, to send

mano (f.) [MAH-noh] hand

manta (f.) [MAHN-tah]
blanket

mantequilla (f.) [mahn-teh-
KEE-yah] butter

manzana (f.) [mahn-SAH-
nah] apple

maquillaje (m.) [mah-kee-
YAH-heh] makeup

mar (m.) [mahr] ocean

marca (f.) [MAR-kah] brand
name

mariscos (m. pl.) [mah-REES-
kohs] seafood

marrón [mah-RROHN]
brown

martes (m.) [MAHR-tehs]
Tuesday

marzo [MAHR-soh] March

más [mahs] more

mayo [MAH-yoh] May

mayonesa (f.) [mah-yoh-NEH-
sah] mayonnaise

medianoche (f.) [meh-dee-
yah-NOH-cheh] midnight

medicamento (m.) [meh-dee-
kah-MEHN-toh] medicine

médico(a) [MEH-dee-koh
(kah)] doctor

medio(a) [MEH-dee-yoh
(yah)] half

mediodía (m.) [meh-dee-yoh-
DEE-yah] noon

menos [MEH-nohs] less

mensaje (m.) [mehn-SAH-heh] message

mercado (m.) [mehr-KAH-doh] market

mermelada (f.) [mehr-meh-LAH-dah] jelly

mes (m.) [mehs] month

mesa (f.) [MEH-sah] table

metro (m.) [MEH-troh] subway

miércoles (m.) [mee-YEHR-koh-lehs] Wednesday

mil [meel] thousand

minusválido(a) [mee-noos-BAH-lee-doh (dah)] handicapped

mirar [mee-RAHR] to look at

moneda (f.) [moh-NEH-dah] change (coins)

morado(a) [moh-RAH-doh (dah)] purple

mostaza (f.) [mohs-TAH-sah] mustard

mostrar [mohs-TRAHR] to show

muestra (f.) [MWEHS-trah] sample

museo (m.) [moo-SEH-yoh] museum

muy [mwee] very

nadie [NAH-dee-yeh] nobody

naranja (f.) [nah-RAHN-hah] orange (fruit)

necesitar [neh-seh-see-TAHR] to need

negro(a) [NEH-groh (grah)] black

noche (f.) [NOH-cheh] evening

norte (m.) [NOHR-teh] north

noticias (f. pl.) [noh-TEE-see-yahs] news

noventa [noh-BEHN-tah] ninety

noviembre [noh-bee-YEHM-breh] November

nueve [NWEH-beh] nine

nuevo(a) [NWEH-boh (bah)] new

número (m.) [NOO-meh-roh] number

ochenta [oh-CHEHN-tah] eighty

ocho [OH-choh] eight

octubre [ohk-TOO-breh] October

oeste (m.) [oh-WEHS-teh] west

oficina (f.) [oh-fee-SEE-nah] office

oír [oy-EER] to hear

ojo (m.) [OH-hoh] eye

once [OHN-seh] eleven

ordenador (m.) [ohr-deh-nah-DOHR] computer

oreja (f.) [oh-REH-hah] ear

oro (m.) [OH-roh] gold

oscuro(a) [oh-SKOO-roh (rah)] dark

otoño (m.) [oh-TOH-nyoh] autumn

otro(a) [OH-troh (trah)] another

padre (m.) [PAH-dreh] father

padres (m. pl.) [PAH-drehs] parents

pagar [pah-GAHR] to pay

país (m.) [pahy-EES] country

pan (m.) [pahn] bread

panadería (f.) [pah-nah-deh-REE-yah] bakery

pantalones (m. pl.) [pahn-tah-LOH-nehs] pants

pañuelo (m.) *de papel* [pah-nyoo-WEH-loh deh pah-PEHL] tissue

papa (f.) [PAH-pah] potato

papel (m.) [pah-PEHL] paper

paquete (m.) [pah-KEH-teh] package

para [PAH-rah] for

parada (f.) *de autobús* [pah-RAH-dah deh ow-toh-BOOS] bus stop

parada (f.) *de taxi* [pah-RAH-dah deh TAHK-see] taxi stand

paraguas (m.) [pah-RAH-gwahs] umbrella

pardo(a) [PAHR-doh (dah)] brown

parque (m.) [PAHR-keh] park

pasado(a) [pah-SAH-doh (dah)] last

pasar [pah-SAHR] to spend time

pasta (f.) *dentífrica* [PAHS-tah dehn-tee-FREE-kah] toothpaste

pastel (m.) [pahs-TEHL] cake

pastilla (f.) [pahs-TEE-yah] pill

pavo (m.) [PAH-boh] turkey

pedir [peh-DEER] to ask

pedir prestado [peh-DEER prehs-TAH-doh] to borrow

película (f.) [peh-LEE-koo-lah] movie

pelo (m.) [PEH-loh] hair

pequeño(a) [peh-KEH-nyoh (nyah)] small

percha (f.) [PEHR-chah] hanger

perder [pehr-DEHR] to lose

periódico (m.) [peh-ree-YOH-dee-koh] newspaper

perro (m.) [PEH-rroh] dog

pescadería (f.) [pehs-kah-deh-REE-yah] fish store

pescado (m.) [pehs-KAH-doh] fish

picante [pee-KAHN-teh] spicy

pie (m.) [pee-YEH] foot

piedra (f.) [pee-YEH-drah] stone

pierna (f.) [pee-YEHR-nah] leg

pimienta (f.) [pee-mee-YEHN-tah] pepper

piscina (f.) [pee-SEE-nah] pool

piso (m.) [PEE-soh] floor (story)

planta (f.) *baja* [PLAHN-tah BAH-hah] ground floor

plata (f.) [PLAH-tah] silver

platillo (m.) [plah-TEE-yoh] saucer

plato (m.) [PLAH-toh] plate

playa (f.) [PLAH-yah] beach

pobre [POH-breh] poor

poco(a) [POH-koh (kah)] little

poder [poh-DEHR] able (to be able), can

pollo (m.) [POH-yoh] chicken

poner [poh-NEHR] to put

por [pohr] by, through, for

por favor [pohr fah-BOHR] please

¿por qué? [pohr keh] why

por supuesto [pohr soo-PWEHS-toh] of course

porque [POHR-keh] because

portátil (inalámbrico) [pohr-tah-TEEL] [(ee-nah-LAHM-bree-koh)] laptop (wireless)

postal (m.) [pohs-TAHL] postcard

postre (m.) [POHS-treh] dessert

precio (m.) [PREH-see-yoh] price

preferir [preh-feh-REER] to prefer

pregunta (f.) [preh-GOON-tah] question

preguntar [preh-goon-TAHR] to ask

prestar [prehs-TAHR] to lend

primavera (f.) [pree-mah-BEH-rah] spring

primer(o)(a) [pree-MEHR (pree-MEH-roh) (pree-MEH-rah)] first

pronóstico (m.) [proh-NOHS-tee-koh] weather forecast

pronto [PROHN-toh] soon

propina (f.) [proh-PEE-nah] tip (gratuity)

próximo [PROHK-see-moh] next

puerta (f.) [PWEHR-tah] door, gate

¿qué? [keh] what

querer [keh-REHR] to want

queso (m.) [KEH-soh] cheese

¿quién (es)? [kee-YEHN (kee-YEH-nehs)] who(m)

quince [KEEN-seh] fifteen

quiosco (m.) *de periódicos* [kee-YOHS-koh deh peh-ree-YOH-dee-kohs] newsstand

rebaja (f.) [reh-BAH-hah] discount

receta (f.) [rreh-SEH-tah] prescription

recibir [rreh-see-BEER] to receive

recibo (m.) [rreh-SEE-boh] receipt

recordar [rreh-kohr-DAHR] to remember

reembolso [rreh-yehm-BOHL-soh] refund

refresco (m.) [rreh-FREHS-koh] soda

regresar [rreh-greh-SAHR] to return

reloj (m.) [rreh-LOH] clock, watch

reparar [rreh-pah-RAHR] to repair

revista (f.) [rreh-BEES-tah] magazine

rojo(a) [RROH-hoh (hah)] red

rosado(a) [RROH-sah-doh (dah)] pink

sábado (m.) [SAH-bah-doh] Saturday

saco (m.) [SAH-koh] jacket

sal (f.) [sahl] salt

salida (f.) [sah-LEE-dah] departure, exit, gate

salir [sah-LEER] to go out, to leave

salsa (f.) [SAHL-sah] sauce

salsa de tomate (f.) [SAHL-sah deh toh-MAH-teh] ketchup

seda (f.) [SEH-dah] silk

seguir [seh-GEER] to follow

seis [SEHY-ees] six

sello (m.) [SEH-yoh] stamp

semana (f.) [seh-MAH-nah] week

ser [sehr] to be

servicio (m.) *de limpieza* [sehr-BEE-see-yoh deh leem-pee-YEH-sah] housekeeping service

servicios (m. pl.) [sehr-BEE-see-yohs] bathrooms

servilleta (f.) [sehr-bee-YEH-tah] napkin

sesenta [seh-SEHN-tah] sixty

setenta [seh-TEHN-tah] seventy

siempre [see-YEHM-preh] always

siete [see-YEH-teh] seven

significar [seeg-nee-fee-KAHR] to mean

silla (f.) [SEE-yah] chair

simpático(a) [seem-PAH-tee-koh (kah)] nice

sin [seen] without

sobre [SOH-breh] upon

soltero(a) [sohl-TEH-roh (rah)] single (unmarried)

sombrero (m.) [sohm-BREH-roh] hat

sopa (f.) [SOH-pah] soup

sucio(a) [SOO-see-yoh (yah)] dirty

suéter (m.) [SWEH-tehr] sweater

supermercado (m.) [soo-pehr-mehr-KAH-doh] supermarket

sur (m.) [soor] south

tabaquería (f.) [tah-bah-keh-REE-yah] tobacco store

también [tahm-bee-YEHN] also, too

tarde [TAHR-deh] late

tarde (f.) [TAHR-deh] afternoon

tarifa (f.) [tah-REE-fah] fare

tarjeta (f.) *de crédito* [tahr-HEH-tah deh KREH-dee-toh] credit card

tarjeta (f.) *de débito* [tahr-HEH-tah deh DEH-bee-toh] debit card

tarjeta (f.) *de embarque* [tahr-HEH-tah deh ehm-BAHR-keh] boarding pass

tarjeta (f.) *de presentación* [tahr-HEH-tah deh preh-sehn-tah-see-YOHN] business card

tarjeta (f.) *telefónica* [tahr-HEH-tah teh-leh-FOH-nee-kah] phone card

tasa (f.) *de cambio* [TAH-sah deh KAHM-bee-yoh] exchange rate

taza (f.) [TAH-sah] cup

té (m.) [teh] tea

teatro (m.) [teh-YAH-troh] theater

temprano [tehm-PRAH-noh] early

tenedor (m.) [teh-neh-DOHR] fork

tener [teh-NEHR] to have

tener calor [teh-NEHR kah-LOHR] to be hot (person)

tener dolor (de) [teh-NEHR doh-LOHR (deh)] to have an ache (in)

tener frío [teh-NEHR FREE-yoh] cold, to be cold (person)

tener hambre [teh-NEHR AHM-breh] hungry (to be hungry)

tener lugar [tch NEHR loo-GAHR] to take place

tener prisa [teh-NEHR PREE-sah] hurry (to be in a hurry)

tener que + infinitive [teh-NEHR keh] to have to

tener sed [teh-NEHR sehd] to be thirsty

tener suerte [teh-NEHR SWEHR-teh] lucky (to be lucky)

tenis (m. pl.) [Latin America, South America] [TEH-nees] sneakers

terminar [tehr-mee-NAHR] to end

tiempo (m.) [tee-YEHM-poh] weather, time

tienda (f.) [tee-YEHN-dah] store

tienda (f.) *de recuerdos* [tee-YEHN-dah deh rreh-KWEHR-dohs] souvenir shop

tienda (f.) *de regalos* [tee-YEHN-dah deh rreh-GAH-lohs] gift shop

tienda (f.) *de ropa* [tee-YEHN-dah deh RROH-pah] clothing store

tienda (f.) *de licores* [tee-YEHN-dah deh lee-KOH-rehs] liquor store

tijeras (f. pl.) [tee-HEH-rahs] scissors

tipo (m.) *de cambio* [TEE-poh deh KAHM-bee-yoh] exchange rate

toalla (f.) [toh-WAH-yah] towel

todavía [toh-dah-BEE-yah] still

todo(a) [TOH-doh (dah)] all

tomar [toh-MAHR] to take

trabajar [trah-bah-HAHR] work

traer [trah-YEHR] to bring

traje (m.) *de baño* [trah-HEH deh BAH-nyoh] bathing suit

trece [TREH-seh] thirteen

treinta [TREHYN-tah] thirty

tren (m.) [trehn] train

tres [trehs] three

un, uno, una [oon, OO-noh, OO-nah] a, an, one

usar [OO-sahr] to use

vaso (m.) [BAH-soh] glass

vegano(a) [beh-GAH-noh (nah)] vegan

vegetariano(a) [beh-heh-tah-ree-YAH-noh (nah)] vegetarian

vehículo (m.) *compartido* [beh-EE-koo-loh kohm-pahr-TEE-doh] rideshare

veinte [BEHYN-teh] twenty

vendedor(a) [behn-deh-DOHR] [(behn-deh-DOH-rah)] salesperson

vender [behn-DEHR] to sell

venir [beh-NEER] to come

venta (f.) [BEHN-tah] sale (bargain)

ventana (f.) [behn-TAH-nah] window

ventanilla (f.) [behn-tah-NEE-yah] car window

ver [behr] to see

verano (m.) [beh-RAH-noh] summer

verde [BEHR-deh] green

verdura (f.) [behr-DOO-rah] vegetable

vestido (m.) [behs-TEE-doh] dress

viajar [bee-yah-HAHR] to travel

viaje (m.) [bee-YAH-heh] trip

viejo(a) [BEE-yeh-hoh (hah)] old

viernes (m.) [bee-YEHR-nehs] Friday

vino (m.) [BEE-noh] wine

viuda (viudo) [bee-YOO-dah (doh)] widow(er)

vivir [bee-BEER] to live

volver [bohl-BEHR] to return

vuelo (m.) [BWEH-loh] flight

ya [yah] already

zapatería (f.) [sah-pah-teh-REE-yah] shoe store

zapatillas (f. pl.) [Spain] sah-pah-TEE-yahs sneakers

zapato (m.) [sah-PAH-toh] shoe

zumo (m.) [Spain] [SOO-moh] juice

Vocabulary Distinctions

Spanish is the native language of about 450 million people and it's the official language of 20 countries and the commonwealth of Puerto Rico. Naturally, throughout the Spanish-speaking world, there are variations in pronunciation as well as regional vocabulary differences. The following pages list some common English words and their equivalents in Spain and other Spanish-speaking countries.

apartment	*el piso* [Spain] ehl PEE-soh
	el departamento, el apartamento [Latin America] ehl deh-pahr-tah-MEHN-toh, ehl ah-pahr-tah-MEHN-toh
Band-Aid	*la tirita* [Spain] lah tee-REE-tah
	la curita [Latin America] lah koo-REE-tah
barbecue	*la barbacoa, la parrilla* [universal] lah bahr-bah-KOH-wah, lah pah-RREE-yah
	el asado [Argentina] ahl ah-SAH-doh
bathing suit	*el bañador, el traje de baño* [universal] ehl bah-nyah-DOHR, ehl TRAH-heh deh BAH-nyoh
	la malla [Argentina] lah MAH-yah
bus	*el autobús* [universal] ehl ow-toh-BOOS
	el camión [Mexico] ehl kah-mee-YOHN
	el colectivo [Argentina] ehl koh-lehk-TEE-boh
cake	*el pastel, el bizcocho* [universal] ehl pahs-TEHL, ehl bees-KOH-choh
	la tarta [Spain] lah TAHR-tah
	la torta [South America] lah TOHR-tah

car	*el coche* [Spain] ehl KOH-cheh
	el carro [Latin America] ehl KAH-rroh
	el auto [Argentina] ehl OW-toh
cell phone	*el móvil* [Spain] ehl MOH-beel
	el celular [Latin America] ehl seh-loo-LAHR
computer	*el ordenador* [Spain] ehl ohr-deh-nah-DOHR
	la computadora [Latin America] lah kohm-poo-tah-DOH-rah
earrings	*los aretes* [universal] lohs ah-REH-tehs
	los pendientes [Spain] lohs pehn-dee-YEHN-tehs
elevator	*el ascensor* [universal] ehl ah-sehn-SOHR
	el elevador [Latin America] ehl eh-leh-bah-DOHR
eyeglasses	*las gafas* [Spain] lahs GAH-fahs
	los lentes [Mexico] lohs LEHN-tehs
	los anteojos [Argentina] lohs ahn-teh-OH-hohs
	los espejuelos [Puerto Rico] lohs ehs-peh-HWEH-lohs

continues

flip-flops	*las chancletas* [universal] lahs chahn-KLEH-tahs
	las chanclas [Spain] lahs CHAHN-klahs
gas station	*la gasolinera* [Spain] lah gah-soh-lee-NEH-rah
	la estación de servicio [Argentina] lah ehs-tah-see-YOHN deh sehr-BEE-see-yoh
green beans	*las habichuelas* [universal] lahs ah-bee-CHWEH-lahs
	las judías [Spain] lahs hoo-DEE-yahs
	los ejotes [Mexico] lohs eh-HOH-tehs
jacket	*la chaqueta* [universal] lah chah-KEH-tah
	el saco [Latin America] ehl SAH-koh
	la campera [Argentina] lah kahm-PEH-rah
juice	*el zumo* [Spain] ehl SOO-moh
	el jugo [Latin America] ehl HOO-goh
peanut	*el cacahuete* [Spain] ehl kah-kah-HWEH-teh
	el cacahuate [Mexico] ehl kah-kah-HWAH-teh
	el maní [Latin America] ehl mah-NEE

potato	*la patata* [universal] lah pah-TAH-tah *la papa* [Latin America] lah PAH-pah
purse	*la cartera* [universal] lah kahr-TEH-rah *la bolsa* [Mexico] lah BOHL-sah
refrigerator	*el refrigerador* [universal] ehl rreh-free-heh-rah-DOHR *la heladera* [Argentina] la eh-lah-DEH-rah *la nevera* [Central America] lah neh-BEH-rah
restroom	*los servicios* [Spain] lohs sehr-BEE-see-yohs *los baños* [Latin America] lohs BAH-nyohs
sack	*el saco* [universal] ehl SAH-koh *el bulto* [Colombia, Ecuador] ehl BOOL-toh
sandwich	*el sándwich* [universal] ehl SAHND-weech *el bocadillo* [Spain] ehl boh-kah-DEE-yoh
sidewalk	*la acera* [universal] lah ah-SEH-rah *la banqueta* [Mexico] lah bahn-KEH-tah
sneakers	*las zapatillas* [Spain] lahs sah-pah-TEE-yahs *los tenis* [Spanish America] lohs TEH-nees

continues

socks	*los calcetines* [Spain] lohs kahl-seh-TEE-nehs
	las medias [Latin America] lahs MEH-dee-yahs
soda	*el refresco* [universal] ehl rreh-FREHS-koh
	la gaseosa [Latin America] lah gah-seh-YOH-sah
stamp	*el sello* [universal] ehl SEH-yoh
	el timbre [Mexico, Central America] ehl TEEM-breh
strawberry	*la fresa* [Spain] lah FREH-sah
	la frutilla [South America] lah froo-TEE-yah
suitcase	*la maleta* [Spain] lah mah-LEH-tah
	la valija [Argentina] lah bah-LEE-hah
	el velís [Mexico] ehl beh-LEES
sweater	*el suéter, el pulóver* [universal] ehl SWEH-tehr, ehl poo-LOH-behr
	el jersey [Spain] ehl JEHR-see
swimming pool	*la piscina* [universal] lah pee-SEE-nah
	la alberca [Mexico] lah ahl-BEHR-kah
T-shirt	*la camiseta* [Spain] lah kah-mee-SEH-tah
	la playera [Mexico] lah plah-YEH-rah

ticket	*el billete, la entrada* [universal] ehl bee-YEH-teh, lah ehn-TRAH-dah *el boleto* [Mexico] ehl boh-LEH-toh
tire (car)	*el neumático, la goma* [universal] ehl neh-yoo-MAH-tee-koh, lah GOH-mah *la llanta* [Latin America] lah YAHN-tah
waiter	*el camarero* [universal] ehl kah-mah-REH-roh *el mesero* [Latin America] ehl meh-SEH-roh *el mozo* [Argentina] ehl MOH-soh
wallet	*la cartera* [universal] lah kahr-TEH-rah *la billetera* [Argentina] lah bee-yeh-TEH-rah

Index